RACE AND THE BLACK–WHITE ACHIEVEMENT GAP MYTH

ATTAINING EQUITY FOR THE AFRICAN AMERICAN LEARNER IN AMERICAN PUBLIC SCHOOLS

*

BY

DR. DARRELL A. JACKSON

Dartoni Press

Hamilton, New Jersey

To

My dear wife, Dr. Tulane N. Ganges Jackson

Our children, Corey Woodson and Kamilah Jackson Woodson, Corey, Jr. and Kaylie Woodson

My parents, Horace and Edith Jackson

And

All the vulnerable children who need a voice as they traverse America's educational institutions

***

Copyright © 2015 by Darrell A. Jackson, Ed.D
Published by Dartoni Press, 6 Stratton Drive, Hamilton Square, New Jersey 08690

Race and the Black White Achievement Gap Myth

ISBN – 978-0-692-50112-2

TABLE OF CONTENTS

INTRODUCTION..page 4

Chapter 1: The Achievement Gap: Correlates and Perspectives..page 11

Chapter 2: The Achievement Gap and Racial Separation in America...page 34

Chapter 3: Adults, School Governance, and the Gap......page 57

Chapter 4:   Segregation Inside the Schoolhouse..........page 78

Chapter 5: Reconfiguring American Schools for Equity and Equality..page 111

References...page 133

INTRODUCTION

> There is no issue that is more volatile, passionate, confusing, perplexing, and complex than the reality of race in America.
> - *Roland S. Martin, CNN political analyst*

Dialog on issues related to race in America is a delicate matter. Historically, Blacks and Whites have not been fully comfortable with each other to the point of being able to have open and honest, productive discourse on race issues and their solutions. Our past provides painful evidence that every widespread gain in race relations is soon trailed by an equally widespread setback that nearly returns the social relationship to square one. A prime example lies in the public school desegregation mandate of the 1954 Brown v. Board of Ed. Supreme Court Decision (americanhistory.si.edu).

The Brown case consolidated petitions filed in several states going back as far as 1951 seeking to remedy the deplorable public school conditions endured by African American children under the "separate but equal" doctrine employed largely in southern states (brownvboard.org/summary/). The Supreme Court's final judgment on implementation of the decision came in 1955. Yet, despite the "with all deliberate speed" language therein, implementation took 20 years to become a significant reality. In 20 more years, American schools were largely resegregated (civilrightsproject.ucla.edu).

In 1903, Black literary and social icon W.E.B. DuBois wrote in <u>The Souls of Black Folks</u>:

> "...the problem of the twentieth century is the problem of the color line."

More than one hundred years later we find that same line between Black and White Americans is still the problem that will not go away. The masses of Blacks and Whites do not live in the same communities, worship in the same churches, or send their children to the same schools. Plans that propose to reinvent race relations have been patronizing and disingenuous, as evidenced by the fact that efforts at changing this age old pattern have been to little avail.

On a national level, time has yielded countless litmus tests of our yet-to-be-healed Black-White adversarial relationship. These periodic social indicators resurface to confirm that scars remain of wounds produced in the country's formative centuries: Jim Crow laws and the rise of the KKK in the late 19th century; the numerous, senseless, public lynchings of innocent Black men throughout the 19th and early-to-mid 20th centuries; the Tulsa, Oklahoma race riot of 1921; and segregation of the United States Armed Services through World War II.

In the latter half of the twentieth century, one hundred years after the Emancipation Proclamation, the convulsions continued with the infamous March 7, 1965, Bloody Sunday attack on peaceful civil rights demonstrators by armed officers on the Edmund Pettus Bridge near Selma, Alabama; the assassination of Martin Luther King and the ensuing riots of the late 1960s; the 1988 subliminally racist Willie Horton metaphor created by the George H.W. Bush campaign; the 1992 Rodney King beating by LAPD officers, the verdict and ensuing riot; and the divergent reactions along racial lines to the 1995 and 1997 criminal and civil trials of O.J. Simpson.

One of the most profound symbols of entrenched American racial intolerance came in the form of the contentious, race-laced 2006-2008 presidential campaign and election of Barack Obama. A poll taken at that time determined that 1 in 5 white Pennsylvanians would not vote for Mr. Obama solely due to his race. Even after his election, many Americans never digested the fact that a Black man (actually half Black) was president of their country. Their hopes rested on the "birther" movement which, in a last ditch, pathetically desperate but ultimately futile strategy, sought to remove the president from office. By 2011, the birthers had yet to give up the fight. And the beat goes on; all this despite present blind-eye claims that American society is post-racial.

In recent years, political correctness has coaxed our culture toward an increasingly more civil tone in manifestations of Black and White differences. But obscured underlying embers continue to smolder as the masses of Black Americans press their noses against the glass of mainstream White American society. Blacks' marginalized condition especially holds true for American public schools, which provide a mirror image of the hearts and minds of the environments in which they exist and of which they are a part.

Just as the separation of Black and White in our greater society is ultimately about race and racism, it is similarly so in the classrooms of our public schools, where history testifies to persistent disparities in learning outcomes between Black and White children. This tendency to sort the races in American schools, the conspiratorial use of pseudo-science to rationalize this dual system, the widespread stereotyping and stigmatization of young Black learners, and the resultant preordained achievement test score differences are the complex and deep-rooted substance of the achievement gap and the focus of this book.

It is because of the emotion that the subject of race evokes that I wish to implore an open-mindedness from all who contemplate the issues examined, hypotheses advanced, and opinions expressed in this book. Above all, I wish for the reader to know that those who perpetuate the conditions that nourish the Black-White achievement gap and racial inequity in our schools are by no means all White. Nor are those who have taken up the struggle for equity and equality in our schools all Black. Prejudice, ignorance, incompetence, and apathy dwell in all races just as impartiality, enlightenment, capability, and sincerity can too be found. Moreover, as phenomenal as it may seem to the average White American, intra-racial bias is not uncommon among African Americans. Just as many Blacks in apartheid South Africa reveled in and exploited their "honorary White" status, numerous black Americans have found over the years that there exists in American culture a career niche for Blacks who will turn a blind eye to injustice or even repress other Blacks at the behest of white employers.

Educating Black children is not about turning sows' ears into silk purses. The problem is not the children. The achievement gap can only be narrowed by educators first abandoning fundamental negative assumptions and beliefs about Black children; then identifying, exposing, and reorienting unequal educational policies and practices that hamstring these children academically. With policies and regulations in place that promote equal opportunity for learning, retraining and results-based accountability for adults in public schools must follow. Ultimately, it is imperative to remove any and all tangible and intangible structures that are obstacles to equal opportunity for all children in our schools.

The approach taken in writing this book is eclectic. Education is a scholarly realm and thus a scholarly format is undertaken in presenting and analyzing theory, facts, statistics, and research findings. However, I find there can be a certain absence of texture and color, a staidness, when assuming a purely scholarly format in writing about the lives of people, especially children. Public education, contrary to the actions of too many adults in the profession, is about flesh and blood clients, the students. Therefore, I believe that capturing the essence of the impact of public education on them entails attention to the affective aspect of children's experiences in our schools. Thus, anecdotes recounting experiences with some of my former students will juxtapose and breathe life into scholarly passages in the ensuing chapters.

Finally, I will also present first person accounts of research, formal and informal, conducted over the years since I taught my first class in 1972. I've long endorsed using the classroom as a laboratory in which prior knowledge and research findings are used in cyclical fashion in the never ending quest to find "what works." This approach (as teacher, principal, and researcher) has led me to discoveries that have been both fruitful to my students and greatly fulfilling to me. It has been the primary vehicle in which I've led the way to higher test scores for my students of all races and a narrowing of the achievement gap in every school in which I've worked.

The title of this book derives from the notion that the Black-White achievement gap, as we call it, is race-based and facilitated/created by adult actors within and outside public schools. In itself, the test score gap is a differential measure of what some students know and others don't know. That this indicator is used to assess educational efficacy of schools is disingenuous and diversionary. It is as if children are the only human factors in the teaching and learning process. Yet they are the primary ones to unjustly bear the brunt of a systemic lack of efficacy. This point is buried in the aftermath of standardized tests as students are the only stakeholders tested and the primary ones punished for poor performance on these tests.

Standardized tests –formerly ASK, HSPA, AP, and SAT in New Jersey - are referred to as "high stakes tests." It is a most accurate and ominous phrase, for these test scores and related content knowledge greatly impact children's short and long term futures. On the line are which courses they'll be placed in; which academic tracks they'll be assigned to; whether or not they'll be relegated to advanced curricula or be assigned to the academic black holes of special education or basic skills (whatever is drawn in never comes out); whether they graduate and which colleges will accept them; whether or not they'll be eligible for scholarship monies; and, ultimately, the quality and gainfulness of their future employment. Indeed, "high stakes" is an understatement for the masses of America's Black children as the test scores associated with each individual will follow him or her in perpetuity.

But there is no individualized, formal, publicized, government-endorsed measure that focuses on teacher and administrator proficiency or lack thereof; and no number in a file that memorializes marginal skills. In fact, at this writing, teachers' unions and administrators have fought achievement-related accountability tooth and nail. Presently, tenured teachers remain employed no matter how poorly their students do. And incompetent non-tenured teachers can pack up and take their certificates to any other district that will hire them. Provided they have favorable references (the sending districts are likely all too happy to endorse and support their departure) they are free to carry their marginal skills to other districts and children.

Thus, using only students' test scores as indicators of efficacy camouflages, protects, and gives anonymity to the adults responsible for producing the substandard product. In fact, my experience has been that most schools would be hard pressed to statistically quantify a given teacher's competence or incompetence in terms of academic value added to their students over time. Yet, for those teachers and administrators there are no high stakes tests. For them there are no stigma-laden, career debilitating test scores in their files. They are one half of a paradoxical system that stigmatizes the client for the incompetence, indifference, and/or negligence of the education practitioner. The ensuing pages will justify this harsh criticism of our misguided system of educational measurement that indirectly blames the victim for its shortcomings.

    I once read that in some ancient literature, critically important concepts were repeated seven times in the writing. One of those crucial concepts to be reiterated herein is that the vast majority of American teachers are phenomenal as people and greatly dedicated to the academic and personal well-being of their students. Thus, it is my intent to create for the reader a mental dichotomy of competent versus incompetent adult educational practitioners. Amidst the occasional passionate, seemingly harsh criticism of those who cavalierly fail to prepare our children for life via education, please pay equal attention to the praise given to some of the most masterful educators it has been my honor to meet and lead.

CHAPTER 1:

BLACK STUDENT UNDERACHIEVEMENT: CORRELATES AND PERSPECTIVES

> Explanations for the achievement gap have spanned between what race scholar Cornell West calls conservative behaviorism and liberal structuralism. Those falling in the first category explain the achievement gap in terms of personal responsibility, citing cultural deficits such as an impoverished work ethic passed on to children by their parents. Those in the latter camp find behavioral factors insufficient, instead explaining this phenomenon as an effect of racism at both an individual and institutional level. *-Niral Shah, University of California, Berkeley*

Quantifying the Gap

Troubling to informed educators and fair-minded Americans has been the persistent Black-White test score gap. A large percentage of African-American students in U.S. schools continually lags behind their European-American counterparts in measures of academic achievement. This test score gap can be seen in mathematics, reading, science, social studies, and virtually all other subject areas (Ferguson, 2002; Thernstrom & Thernstrom, 2003). Although National Assessment of Educational Progress (NAEP) data indicate that gains have been made and the gap has narrowed in certain time periods, little progress has been made since 1990 in bringing Black American public school students' average academic achievement indicators closer to that of White students.

Table 1 illustrates the percent of American public school thirteen year-olds by race who scored at or above the National Assessment of Educational Progress (NAEP) level 150 in reading proficiency in selected test years. That level is the lowest on the NAEP scale and is defined as one's ability to follow brief written directions and to carry out simple, discrete reading tasks (nces.ed.gov).

Table 1
Percent of American Thirteen Year-Old Students at or Above NAEP Level 150 Reading Proficiency by Race for Selected Years

	1971	1975	1980	1984	1988	1990	1992
Black	98.6	98.4	99.3	99.4	99.8	99.4	98.7
White	99.9	99.9	100	99.9	99.9	99.9	99.8
Hisp.	N/A	99.6	99.7	99.9	99.2	99.1	98.1

The table clearly shows that in the years between 1971 and 1992, there was virtually no difference among Black, White, and Hispanic students at the *lowest* reading proficiency level. During that time, the vast majority of all thirteen year-olds in American public schools demonstrated at least minimum literacy by NAEP standards.

Table 2
Percent of American Thirteen Year-Old Students at or Above NAEP Level 250 Reading Proficiency by Race for Selected Years

	1971	1975	1980	1984	1988	1990	1992
Black	21.1	24.8	30.1	34.6	40.2	41.7	38.4
White	64.2	65.5	67.8	65.3	63.7	64.8	68.5
Hisp.	N/A	32.0	35.4	39.0	38.0	37.2	40.9

Table 2 illustrates percentages of the three racial groups scoring 250 or higher in reading proficiency. The National Assessment of Educational Progress places students' test scores into five levels beginning at 150 and in increments of 50 up to 350, which is the highest level. The middle reading proficiency level, 250, is defined as being able to search for specific information, interrelate ideas, and to make generalizations about literature, science, and social studies materials.

Whereas level 200 reading scores demonstrate higher literacy than level 150, level 250 is particularly significant because it is the first NAEP level where proficiency is defined in terms of ability to function well in the curricular content areas (nces.ed.gov) and thus succeed academically at the secondary level. It is at this level that the gap becomes pronounced between Black, White, and Hispanic thirteen year old school children. Indeed, in four of the six selected years in which NAEP data were gathered on Hispanic literacy, the percentage of Hispanic thirteen year old American public school students scoring at the 250 level surpassed the percentage of Black students at that level. Further review of NAEP reading, math, and writing tables demonstrates that a statistically significant gap exists between Black and White thirteen year olds at all proficiency levels between 250 and 350. The gap increases exponentially as the levels increase beyond 250.

If the above differences in mean national test scores present a stark contrast of Black and White academic achievement for middle school-age students, the problem is all the more telling when examined by geographic regions of the United States. Table 3 displays demographic and achievement gap data from two Northern states, New Jersey and New York, and two Southern states, Mississippi and North Carolina.

[nces.ed.gov/programs/digest/d09/tables/dt09_122.asp]

Table 3
Student Population Racial Breakdown and Percent Below Grade 8 Basic Reading Proficiency for Two Northern and Two Southern States in Year 2001-2002

	% Black	% White	% Below Basic Proficiency Black	White
Mississippi	50.7	47.3	56	23
New York	19.7	53.9	49	13
New Jersey	17.7	57.9	38	12
No. Carolina	31.6	58.3	51	21

Some might find it surprising that the Black-White achievement gap is larger in New York than it is in Mississippi and North Carolina in terms of the percentage of eighth graders below

NAEP basic reading proficiency indicators. These data also underscore the fact that by disaggregating the NAEP national mean data, one sees that the achievement gap is more severe in some states and geographic regions than the averaged national data might imply.

Overall, examination of NAEP achievement test scores shows that Black middle school students continue to lag behind their White counterparts, thus presenting a troubling prospect for their life chances should the condition perpetuate. Placed in an economic context, most inner city teenagers who attain no higher than 150 level reading proficiency have very real prospects of attaining only the most menial, low-paying jobs. It is likely that they presently live at or below the poverty line and it may well be that in the absence of radical systemic changes in American schools they will remain there or, worse yet, become part of the growing Black underclass.

Myth Perpetuated by Publicizing Gap

Embedded in the concept of chronic disparity in Black-White scholastic achievement is the misguided notion that the two racial populations have performed and continue to perform in grossly different ways on tests that objectively measure knowledge and scholastic cognitive ability. The tests themselves are portrayed as scientific, appropriate in design, psychometrically sound, and objective, i.e. that each student who sits for the test has the same opportunity for success as any other, regardless of race, gender, school district, culture, or socioeconomic status. This is illusory and fundamentally flawed in that we have known for decades that biases can readily be found in all tests that require students to read, interpret, and respond to questions written by test makers who don't necessarily write or speak like them or have similar life experiences (Johnston, P., 1984).

We also know that teaching methods, classroom dynamics, and related learning vary from district to district, school to school, and even classroom to classroom within schools. Yet standardized tests only indirectly measure what districts, schools, and teachers do and test score reporting is not specific to those entities. Rather, test scores are reported in terms of student outcomes, i.e. what knowledge and ability the student is able (or not able) to demonstrate. Thus, the sensibilities of readers of test scores may be guided toward the misconception that the achievement gap is a measure of innate Black-White differences. And readers of all races may well interpret this to mean that once again, the Jaquans and the Shanequas of the many Philadelphias (Mississippi or Pennsylvania), Camdens (New Jersey or South Carolina), and Trentons (North Carolina or New Jersey) have demonstrated what we've long suspected: no amount of money can educate the uneducable.

The gap conceptually seems to say that post-Brown Decision American schools have placed Black and White students side by side in the classroom, exposed them to the same curricula, and provided them with qualified teachers only to produce decade upon decade of divergent learning outcomes. This deficit view of African American students that Americans have long internalized belies the fact that no credible research has identified innate differences in intelligence between Black and White children. Indeed, on this subject, noted scholar Ashley Montagu writes:

> "What is "intelligence?" The answer most people would give to that question would be, "What IQ tests measure." … IQ tests, whatever their proponents may claim, do not

measure intelligence. The truth is that no one really knows what the structure of intelligence is, and therefore there cannot be anything even approximating a quantitative measure of intelligence, this abstraction of abstractions, that IQ tests purport to quantify. What is quite clear, except to IQ testers, is that many conditions enter into the making of the capabilities we call intelligence, and that without taking these factors into consideration such tests are quite valueless in providing a measure of "intelligence." (Montagu, 1999)

My purpose for writing this book is to present an alternative argument for the origins of what we call the Black-White student achievement gap and reasons for its persistence. More succinctly, I propose that contrary to the long-standing, thinly veiled notion in American society that the masses of Black children are less intellectually capable of scholastic success than White children, the fact is that policies, practices, attitudes, and behaviors commonly emanating from the adults who directly or indirectly run American schools create disparate learning sub-environments that preordain divergent scholastic outcomes for Black and White students.

When considered in this context, the achievement gap is actually a summative measure of the poor quality of students' educational inputs rather than being a testament to any academic or intellectual shortcomings of Black students. Note that test scores of individual students as well as population subgroups only state what the *student* can demonstrate vis a vis the learning/teaching process, as if the student is autonomous, self-taught, and the only factor in his or her education. With the adult professional factors glaringly absent from reported test scores, one is unable to identify specific groups of teachers and other adults who failed to provide the essential inputs necessary for higher learning levels and commensurate assessment results.

Gap's Toll on Human Capital

The achievement gap is about what has happened and continues to happen in urban, suburban, and rural public schools to America's most precious commodity: our children. Given that, later chapters will vividly reveal anecdotal accounts of the public school experiences of children I have known as a professional educator. My hope is that in reading these stories, the reader will be left with a rightfully poignant picture of children who enter kindergarten wide-eyed and eager to learn, only to become disillusioned and inculcated with a sense of failure and second-class citizenship by the time they leave elementary school.

One alarming indicator of internalized sense of academic futility borne by African American high school students is the true rate at which they drop out of school. According to a 2007 report by James J. Heckman of the University of Chicago and Paul A. LaFontaine of the American Bar Association, the true American high school graduation rate is substantially lower than the official rate reported by the National Center for Educational Statistics. They found that the graduation rate has been decreasing over the past 40 years and the minority graduation rate has not tended toward the White rate over the past 35 years. According to the report, more than one third of Black and Hispanic students leave school before graduation (Heckman, J.J. & LaFontaine, P.A., 2007).

Historical Foundation for Black Underachievement

Social scientists have identified certain social conditions in America as precursors to Black underachievement. Racial segregation and segregated schools have been proven to be major contributors to the problem due to accompanying inadequate funding for predominantly Black schools, lower teacher quality, and inadequate resources as compared to White schools (Franklin, 1967; Simpson & Yinger, 1972). These factors conspired to inhibit academic success and diminish the life chances of Black children (Jencks, 1972).

De jure segregation of schools effectively institutionalized racial separation for more than the first half of the twentieth century, making educational progress for Blacks difficult at best (LaMorte, 2002). In 1896, the United States Supreme Court handed down the now-famous Plessy v. Ferguson decision that gave states the right to provide "separate but equal" schools for Black and White children.

The Plessy case stemmed from an 1890 Jim Crow law passed by the Louisiana legislature that required separate rail car accommodations for Black and White railway passengers. Homer Plessy, a Black man, protested the law by riding in the "Whites only" car and was subsequently arrested (socialstudieshelp.com). The Court heard the case and ruled in favor of the State, noting that the Constitution guaranteed Blacks the right to equal facilities as Whites but not the *same* facilities. Justice Henry Brown, in writing for the majority, held that:

> "Laws permitting, and even requiring, their separation (of Blacks and Whites) in places where they are liable to be brought into contact do not necessarily imply the inferiority of either race to the other, and have been generally, if not universally, recognized as within the competency of the state legislatures in the exercise of their police power. The most common instance of this is connected with the establishment of separate schools for white and colored children, which has been held to be a

valid exercise of the legislative power even by courts of States where the political rights of the colored race have been longest and most earnestly enforced."

He further held that the contested Jim Crow law "neither abridges the privileges or immunities of the colored man, deprives him of his property without due process of law, nor denies him the equal protection of the laws within the meaning of the Fourteenth Amendment." (Plessy v. Ferguson, Supreme Court of the United States, 1896 163 U.S. 537).

The Plessy decision's endorsement of segregated schools opened the door for states to more broadly apply the separate-but-equal doctrine ((Franklin, 1967; LaMorte, 2002; Simpson & Yinger, 1972). The practice was protected by law until 1954 when the United States Supreme Court handed down the historic Brown v. Board of Education decision, thereby rendering de jure segregated public schools unconstitutional in America. Yet, nearly four decades after that decision, urban public school students were still racially isolated, with non-Asian minorities comprising the vast majority of the populations of America's eight largest cities. In 1990, African Americans comprised only 8.7% of suburban residents surrounding twelve major metropolitan areas and more than half of the population of New York City, Chicago, Los Angeles, Atlanta, Detroit, and Miami. In one of those areas, Newark, New Jersey, 22% of the residents had less than a ninth grade education and only 51.2% graduated from high school (Anyon, 1997).

Though some progress had been made in the last half of the twentieth century in deceasing racial separation in American schools, these statistics indicate that desegregation as a means of increasing achievement levels for African Americans has often been followed by resegregation. And while excellence in predominately poor and Black schools is a possibility, the history of public education in this period strongly suggests that such schools are far from the norm (Thernstrom & Thernstrom, 2003). It also suggests that attacking the achievement gap by changing the socioeconomic landscape is a formidable undertaking. Through the decade of the 1990's, African American children from kindergarten to college continued to score lower on mathematics, reading, and other achievement tests as compared with their White American counterparts (Jencks & Phillips, 1998).

Micro-environmental Approaches to Addressing the Achievement Gap

First and foremost, efforts to displace centuries of social inertia were bound to require both insight and patience. Decades of work on the social environments of public schools have certainly paved the way for strides in racial equity. But the meager gains in closing the achievement gap compared to the total amount of rhetoric about the gap have created frustration, disappointment, and resignation among educators (Jencks & Phillips, 1998). This quandary underscored the need for researchers to continue to search for other root causes or even the proximate causes of differences in school achievement between Black and White students. Ideally, deeper understanding of the problem could lead to more immediate interventions that are reproducible and sustainable in a variety of academic settings.

A shift in thinking among scholars led to a more recent body of research that turns away from investigations of the macro social environments in which American public schools operate toward more focused studies of internal school environments, home-school interactions, and intra-cultural social interactions (Paschal, Weinstein, & Walberg, 1984; Thernstrom & Thernstrom, 2003). Current researchers seem to favor a pragmatic approach to narrowing the achievement gap by looking for conditions where change is more feasible in the short term and also where reforms can be manipulated and approached at the district, school, and even personal levels (Fehrman, 1987).

Clearly there are multiple cause and effect relationships that are the root causes of Black underachievement (Ferguson, 2002). Underachieving Black middle school students comprise a mass collection of individuals who bring with them a broad array of obstacles to academic success. Some have difficulty forming all-important social relationships, others have dysfunctional home environments, identity issues, and yet others experience anxiety in academic settings. One manifestation of these problems may be what some consider laziness, procrastination, and lack of motivation (Ford, 1996).

Just as no one problem forms the foundation of the Black-White achievement gap, there is no one-size-fits-all intervention that can universally apply to all underachievers (Ford, 1996). To close the Black-White achievement gap, teachers need pragmatic classroom-level interventions that can attract African American students to the educational process by presenting relevant content and appropriate instructional practices. However, a critical first step is building connections between teachers and students (Ferguson, 2002).

The Paradox of High Achievement in Low SES Schools

The long-standing achievement gap at all levels between Black and White students has been widely articulated and examined from the perspective of socioeconomics, culture, inferior schooling, and other social constructs (Cooper, Harris, et al., 1998; Thernstrom & Thernstrom, 2003). Yet socio-economic status (SES), race, culture, and school quality have not been shown to be absolute predictors of achievement test scores. A review of National Assessment of Educational Progress (NAEP) data demonstrates that each year some percentages of Black students are highly successful academically. These year-to-year percentages have been compared to White students' performance but when examined absolutely, they indicate that some African American students, albeit a small number, achieve at high levels in spite of school demographics and race.

If this point is examined in terms of reading achievement, we see nationally that approximately 47% of White and 18% of Black high school seniors from all SES levels scored proficient or advanced in the 1998 NAEP Assessment (Thernstrom & Thernstrom, 2003). While these data have been presented by the authors in the context of *differences* in Black-White achievement, they also illustrate that nearly 20% of Black students from all backgrounds were academically successful in schools in which up to 80% of other Black students from similar backgrounds were not academically proficient by NAEP standards. A view of this phenomenon in settings where poverty and race coexist presents further substantiation of this point.

Existing data show that some Black students can still achieve superior standardized test scores while living in poverty and attending predominantly Black and poor schools (Thernstrom & Thernstrom, 2003). Camden Middle School in Newark, New Jersey, is a school that had a 90% African American student population with 81% receiving free lunch, a standard measure of poverty (www.state.nj.us/education/). The school's 2005 Grade Eight Proficiency Assessment (GEPA) Language Arts Literacy results show that 3.5% of its students scored advanced proficient, which is the highest GEPA achievement level. This compares to only 15.9% of students scoring advanced proficient in the *wealthiest districts* in New Jersey. A better perspective to this paradox may be found in the fact that if reduced to its simplest terms, achievement is a function of doing work: reading, note taking, and other active forms of learning. These are all behaviors that are associated with achievement (Thernstrom & Thernstrom, 2003). It also logically follows that some Black students, even in the most dire of school cultures, execute the behaviors associated with school success and academic achievement. This suggests that positive social and academic transformation of those same cultures would yield favorable results.

Research on Black Student Underachievement

As early as the 1970s, the late educational anthropologist John Ogbu proposed controversial theories about African Americans' relative underachievement that directly challenged certain popular beliefs and theories on the subject. Some of his predecessors and contemporaries had blamed the gaps on institutionalized racism and low expectation (Rosenthal and Jacobson, 1968). Still others located the problem within African Americans themselves, suggesting that they were genetically inferior (Hernnstein, 1973; Jensen, 1969) and culturally deprived (Bloom, Davis, & Hess, 1965). Ogbu's (1978) research indicated that African Americans were not unlike other oppressed minorities in the world, in a caste system that created a socioeconomic hierarchy wherein they were relegated to the lowest positions, inherited the lowest paying jobs, and were generally denied the trappings of more privileged classes. In spite of their low socioeconomic status on average, African Americans were expected to work as hard as those who reaped the greatest economic benefits. Ogbu speculated that in order to alleviate the psychic dissonance created by high expectations and meager rewards, African-Americans rejected a strong academic work ethic as fruitless.

Building upon his earlier research, Ogbu (1981) pioneered a cultural ecological model of race and society. He argued that African Americans have been shut out of mainstream America socially, economically, and educationally and that a multi-generational cycle of frustration conditioned them to seek alternative pathways to social and economic success. According to Ogbu, Blacks may perceive the standard model of hard work and perseverance as a smokescreen for embedded agreements among Whites to favor their own whenever possible. Blacks may then adopt alternative strategies in terms of life style and economic success. These strategies are culturally evolved and oppositional to the mainstream White world (Harpalani & Gunn, 2003). Ogbu portrayed this evolved sense of identity as a device to reduce the stress and anxiety of striving in an educational system designed historically for second-class citizenship.

Ogbu and Fordham (1986) later concluded that Black students had established a unified subculture wherein negative sanctions awaited those members who in any way displayed an affinity for what the subculture identified as White values. Given the subculture's rejection of the majority culture's value of education, this effectively created a self-fulfilling prophecy of underachievement. Attributing value to schooling and academic achievement was judged to be antithetical to the values of the subculture. Ogbu (2003) referred to Black students' rejection of academics as academic disengagement. His research found that Blacks at all economic levels identified with this disengaged subculture.

In a study of schools in the affluent suburb of Shaker Heights, Ohio, Ogbu (2003) found that a disengaged attitude toward school and schooling had developed among the district's

African American students. Manifestations of the attitudes of Black students in Shaker Heights toward white values were behaviors such as rejection of Standard English speech patterns, negative comments about Black students who "talked intelligent," and rejection of the practice of doing homework. The Shaker Heights findings effectively located the problem of academic disengagement across a broad socioeconomic range of people within African American culture, from urban to upper middle class individuals.

Other social scientists have arrived at similar conclusions about Black underachievement using methods that differ from and extend beyond those of Ogbu. Stanford University psychologist Claude Steele (1999) introduced the concept of *stereotype threat* as a possible key to unlocking the puzzle of underachievement among erstwhile high-achieving Black college students in certain testing situations. Stereotype threat refers to a latent awareness of attributes that define a particular stereotype. This awareness remains latent until the person whose social group is the object of the stereotype and is placed in a situation with members of other social groups wherein the threat of confirming the stereotype exists.

In Steele's experiments, Black and White Stanford undergraduate students with similar academic abilities and profiles were given a difficult test and told it was a test of their ability. The results indicated that Black subjects consistently underperformed, and Steele concluded that this occurred because of Black students' fear of being seen as less intelligent than Whites. The experiment was repeated with White and Asian students and the White students scored significantly lower than the Asians. Steele (1999) suggested that policy makers that would like to relieve the negative effects of stereotype threat on performance should rework the social environments of schools so as to foster a genuine climate of fairness. He holds that the very basis of stereotype threat is students' lack of trust in systems they perceive to be racially biased.

Research by Ogbu (1978; 1981; 2003) and Steele (1999) on the Black-White achievement gap strongly implies that many Black students have voluntarily declined to aggressively participate in their education. Ogbu's conclusions have been applied to urban and middle class Black students; Steele's conclusions have been applied to these groups, too, even though Steele's subjects were often financially comfortable, high-level college students. Combined, their work effectively covers the gamut of Black American youth. The work of both scholars points to underlying social structures that are perceived by Black students to be biased, unfair and discouraging of full participation in the educational process. To assume that these theories explain the totality of minority underachievement is to commit a substantial error, as stated by Donna Ford (1996):

> Underachieving students are not a homogeneous group. Some students have problems associated with poor peer or social relationships, identity issues, anxiety, defensiveness, or negative self-esteem. Other students may lack motivation and may be considered lazy, procrastinators, perfectionists, or nonconformists. A common perception is that students would not be underachievers if they would 'just try harder,' 'pay attention,' and 'listen.' However, overcoming or reversing underachievement is not that simple for many students, particularly those who have had little or no early intervention, those who lack basic skills to take advantage of educational opportunities, and those who have negative self-images. (pp. 1-2)

Black Adolescent Peer Culture and Achievement Values

A number of researchers present evidence that an anti-White, unified cultural identity stands as a barrier in the way of Black students' academic achievement (Ferguson, 2002; Ogbu 1978, 1981, 2003; Steele, 1997). However, children's strong racial identity has also been found to be critical to their well-being and is especially important to adolescents as they attempt to rationalize their place in the American social order (Quintana, 1998). Further, unified racial identity can promote and predict academic efficacy in eighth grade Black students if achievement is perceived as an integral component of being Black (Oyserman, 2001).

In a controlled survey of Black inner city adolescent boys and girls (N=91), Oyserman (2001) sought the students' perceptions of their academic efficacy and racial-ethnic identity. In the former category, the instrument measured 6 items on a 5-point Likert scale. The items measured teachers' helpfulness, completed homework, fulfillment of teachers' expectations, and understanding of subject matter. Using a 3-item 5-point Likert scale instrument to survey racial-ethnic identity, students' sense of connectedness to the Black community, awareness of racism, and association of achievement and the Black community were measured.

In the above study, Oyserman (2001) found that when students viewed academic achievement as part of their racial identity, academic efficacy was strengthened. She also found that boys' awareness of racism encouraged their sense of academic efficacy but the opposite effect was found in girls. This may suggest that Black students' sense of racial connectedness and identity can be positive forces in improving achievement if it is internalized as being linked to academic efficacy.

This suggests that Black students need not relinquish the values and beliefs that form their racial identity in order to be academically successful. Rather, inculcation of the value of academic success into Black students' subculture may strengthen their abilities to succeed academically (Oyserman, 2001).

Peer Influence in Academic Socialization

Prior to school entry, parents play the greatest role in shaping children's thoughts, values, and behaviors. But increasingly, from school entry to adolescence, it is usual that peer groups are the most powerful influence in the lives of children (Henry, 2000). Through preschool and kindergarten, children are closely supervised in their social interactions with other children and have fewer opportunities to exercise autonomy in selection of interpersonal interactions and associations. These may be the first regular social experiences they have with children other than family. As they progress into elementary school, middle school, and high school, peer groups gain definition and meaning and cliques are formed based on perceived similarity in characteristics of the members of the group (Henry, Tolan, & Van Acker, 1997).

Through the course of child development from pre-school to adolescence, children's beliefs, attitudes, activities, associations, sense of efficacy, social behaviors, and appearance are influenced by their peers (Brown, 1990; O'Brien & Bierman, 1988). Researchers widely disagree on the nature and sources of influence, good or bad, to which children and adolescents are subjected in their respective stages of development. In the case especially of urban minority adolescents, much research evidence exists that peer influences are often negative and result in self destructive behaviors like violence, delinquency, drinking, smoking, and drug abuse (Dishion, Reid, & Patterson, 1988;

Dishion, Capaldi, Spracklen, & Li, 1995; Hawkins, Catalano, & Miller, 1992; Hawkins, Lishner, & Catalano, 1985). Still others hold that this position oversimplifies children's social leanings, positing instead that they respond to the quality of a number of layered and sequentially experienced social systems including the family, early schooling, school and community, and the macro environment (Bronfenbrenner, 1979).

In a study designed to investigate developmental changes in the perception of peer groups and peer group influence, O'Brien and Bierman (1988) interviewed seventy-two fifth, eight, and eleventh grade girls and boys. The researchers interviewed subjects in two parts. In the first, subjects were asked to list and describe the various types of peer groups in their schools, including features, characteristics, activities, association, appearance, attitudes, and social behaviors. They were then asked five questions designed to elicit their perceptions of the strength and nature of peer group influence.

In the second portion of the interview, students were asked four questions about their perceptions of the emotional impact of peer group acceptance. Responses described a range of emotions including those derived from companionship, entertainment, nurturance, social acceptance or isolation, self-pride, or not being good enough. Subjects' responses to all questions were coded as positive or negative and placed into one of three categories: social support/friendship, social worth, or personal worth (O'Brien & Bierman, 1988).

The results of the study indicated clear developmental differences in preadolescents (fifth graders), early adolescents (eighth graders), and later adolescents (eleventh graders) in their perceptions of peer groups and peer influence. In terms of peer group definition, the fifth grade subjects focused on activities and social behaviors in describing these groups. Eighth and eleventh graders defined their peer groups more by appearance, attitudes, and group interactions. Group influence on individual attitudes increased across grade levels (O'Brien & Bierman, 1988). Regarding subjects' perceptions of the impact of peer acceptance on their emotional well-being, all felt that group support was important. However, peer groups' influence on feelings of personal and social worth increased with grade level.

Some social scientists have posited that African Americans have endured generational cycles of racism and unequal treatment as compared to White Americans (Franklin, 1967; Simpson & Yinger, 1972). The result has been that they have formed a unified subculture that promotes its own set of values and beliefs, rejects values and beliefs perceived to be "White," and imposes sanctions on nonconforming group members (Ogbu, 1978). It therefore holds that where this dynamic is at play, identification with their ethnicity by Black adolescents effectively establishes classmates as members of a peer group (Ogbu, 1978; Lashbrook, 2000). Individual members of that group possess a powerful desire and motivation to conform to the norms of the group and as such are subject to the influence of that group through the mechanisms of perceived peer pressure or peer influence (Scheff, 1990).

This perceived pressure may be manifest in the form of negative emotions such as shame, feelings of inadequacy, and fear of isolation (Lashbrook, 2000). However, it may also be a precursor to positive bonds that support academic achievement among African American children who find themselves in the same educational setting (O'Brien & Bierman, 1988). Research identifies the peer group as an influential agent of academic socialization as adolescents' beliefs, behaviors, and achievement motivation are shaped by their peers (Ryan, 2000).

Summary

Research on the Black-White achievement gap has identified certain social conditions in America as precursors to black underachievement. Racial segregation and segregated schools have been demonstrated to be major contributors to the problem due to inadequate funding for predominantly Black schools, lower teacher quality, and inadequate resources as compared to White schools. Some researchers looked to Black-White relations for causal factors and identified aspects of Black American culture that contribute to underachievement among Black students.

Academic disengagement has characterized many African American students' approach to public schooling. Having undergone generations of assignment to the margins of American society and within the American economy, they adapted by withdrawing from mainstream White values of work ethic and belief in America as a meritocracy (Ogbu, 1978). What resulted was a unified subculture that spanned all economic levels of Black America. At the school level, Black students who identified with the subculture contributed to underachievement of others by ostracizing fellow Blacks who valued scholastic achievement (Ogbu & Fordham, 1981).

The constructs of academic disengagement and stereotype threat strongly suggest that race is a significant component of the self-identity of many Black students. To the extent that value of academic achievement, initiative to succeed in school, and motivation to commit to the behaviors normally associated with scholastic success are lacking as elements of that identity, Black students will continue to contribute to the achievement gap. When viewed at the school and classroom levels, racial self-identity assigns Black students to peer groups according to age level and makes them subject to the influences, positive or negative, of those groups.

The literature on peer influence posits that adolescents form peer groups based on perceived similarities, like race, dress, or activities among group members. Once groups are formed, peer group members desire to be accepted by the group as a whole and perceive emotional pressure to embrace the values and conform to the behavioral norms of the group to maintain that acceptance. This perceived pressure or peer influence is greatest in the adolescent years (Henry, 2000; Henry, Tolan, & Van Acker, 1997). However, peer group values and norms are not static and may evolve in positive or negative directions based on the quality of environmental influences (Bronfenbrenner, 1979).

Cited research suggests that extrinsic reinforcement offered by the teacher may be an environmental element that serves as the tipping point from which Black classroom level peer groups are motivated to reorient themselves to the achievement-related behaviors common to success. The power of peer influence may be one answer to the perennial question of how teachers can motivate disengaged underachieving students to engage in learning behaviors in the manner of high achievers. In this regard, social science icon Dr. James Comer writes:

> "Students' behavior, attitude, and achievement levels are to a large extent influenced by school climate and a strong instructional program rather than by socioeconomic status and ethnic background." (Comer et al, 1996)

CHAPTER 2:

THE ACHIEVEMENT GAP AND RACIAL SEPARATION IN AMERICA

> *There where it is we do not need the wall: He is all pine and I am apple orchard. My apple trees will never get across and eat the cones under his pines, I tell him. He only says, 'Good fences make good neighbors'.*
> *Robert Frost, from <u>Mending Wall</u>*

    The achievement gap myth emanates in large part from the myriad ways America segregates Blacks and Whites. It is an outgrowth of the racial divide embedded in our culture and yet another manifestation of that chasm. In the slavery years, Blacks resided in dwellings that were spatially apart from those of their masters and far inferior in quality and comfort. In this context, little has changed in the present day as the finest and most regally appointed American homes are generally inhabited by Whites and "slum" or "ghetto" is synonymous with urban Black reservations.

    The majority of Blacks and Whites also reside in separate informally assigned sections of cities and suburban areas of many geographic regions. This geographic separation limits intimate interracial interaction and thus aids and abets ignorance of one race about the other. Separated living sustains interracial mistrust and, among Whites, feeds the segregation mind-set by erroneously equating it with safety, security, and property value retention (Wilson, 1998). Recent history and the twentieth century evolution of some major cities serve to underscore and substantiate this point.

A History of Sorting by Race

The decade of the 1960's produced a number of images that are indelibly etched in the memories of Americans who lived during that tumultuous period. One such image was that of Alabama Governor George Wallace confronting Nicholas Katzenbach, the Attorney General of the United States, at the doorway to the University of Alabama administration building. Wallace, under the watchful eye of the entire country, indeed the world, was making good on his promise to the White people of Alabama to block admission of Blacks to that school, adamant that segregation would remain the unwavering social order of the South in perpetuity.

Ironically, George Wallace's now infamous "segregation today...segregation tomorrow...segregation forever" quote came nearly ten years after the United States Supreme Court handed down the Brown v. Board of Education of Topeka Kansas decision, which declared segregation in public schools to be unconstitutional. Despite that ruling, which mandated that American schools be integrated "With all deliberate speed," the force of law was confronted by the recalcitrant will of the people; and the people won in not only southern schools but northern schools as well (www.reuters.com, 2009)

The Black-White achievement gap and segregation are both about race and racism, not perceived inadequacies of Black children. Both are emblematic of America's ongoing resolve to maintain a social hierarchy wherein Whites are perched at the top level and Blacks at the bottom. That separation of the masses of Black and White Americans can be seen in virtually all threads of the American social fabric. It therefore logically holds that even in so-called integrated settings, e.g. public schools, the power of the will to separate the races is manifest in subtle and not-so-subtle ways. This point will be expounded upon later.

In early American history, the fact of racial segregation was obvious and unquestioned, especially during the institution of slavery. But colonial visionaries knew that the days of "the evil institution" were numbered and that provisions for emancipation of Black slaves required considerable deliberation. This was imperative given the long-standing American cultural value of race-based social stratification and the fear that expanding numbers of Blacks induced. Moreover, the prevailing belief among White American citizens and lawmakers was that the well-being of the country depended on a well-crafted long term plan of separation of the races. One influential architect and proponent of post-manumission racial segregation was Thomas Jefferson.

Near the close of the eighteenth century Jefferson, as Governor of Virginia, chose his annual State of the State report as the forum through which to reflect upon and summarize a century and a half of Black-White American race relations. In that report he succinctly articulated a fear-founded, widely held rationale for permanent separation of the races. Jefferson, James Monroe, and others in political power at that time had discussed colonizing freed slaves to some undetermined foreign land and replacing them with equal numbers of White settlers. On this and the subject of emancipation Jefferson wrote:

> "...Advance it therefore as a suspicion only, that the blacks, whether originally a distinct race, or made distinct by time and circumstances, are inferior to the whites in the endowments of body and mind...This unfortunate difference of colour, and perhaps of faculty, is a powerful obstacle to the emancipation of these people. Among the Romans, emancipation required but one effort. The slave, when made free, might mix with, without staining, the

blood of his master. But with us a second is necessary, unknown to history. When freed, he is to be removed beyond the reach of mixture."

Thomas Jefferson, Notes on the State of Virginia 1782

Jefferson's final edict – "When freed, he is to be removed beyond the reach of mixture." - was prophetic and ominous in tone. From the eighteenth century to the present, the progeny of slaves and freed slaves have never known a time when Whites and Blacks were not separated by law or de facto. But the breadth and depth of that segregation could not have been imagined even by such a brilliant, albeit racist, visionary as Jefferson. For just as Jefferson-era slavery presented a fixed social order that was both physical and psychological, as America moved gradually toward manumission, mechanisms were created to maintain that social paradigm. White Americans at all political levels, local to federal, public and clandestine, supported those mechanisms that served to stratify the races.

Segregation in Housing

Schools fundamentally replicate the beliefs and values of the communities and cities in which they exist. The parents and students come from those areas and the boards of education are comprised of adults who live in those communities or cities. It logically follows that the educational policies developed by boards of education are uniquely reflective of the beliefs and values of those individuals and groups. Emphasis on policy is added through input from influential parents and administrators. It is therefore axiomatic that schools socially and politically replicate the environments in which they are situated. It also reasonably holds that segregated communities – those with concentrations of Whites and minorities in given loci – will segregate their schools at some level.

Racial stratification in our schools is a reprehensible but logical extension of the endless list of ways in which Black and White people are physically and psychologically segregated in America. So pervasive and commonplace is this division that we tend to dismiss it as normal. We don't notice it much like we don't notice air even as we are encased in it. Whether intentional or the unwitting outcome of benign tradition, physical and psychological racial segregation perpetuate the notion that ours is a nation begun by and for people of European ancestry and that the best things that America has to offer are available in a pecking order according to that long-established racial hierarchy. This is the element of "White privilege."

Glaringly obvious physical separation of Blacks and Whites can be readily seen as we drive or travel through America's cities and residential communities. In all states and virtually all counties in those states that have diverse populations, one finds significant racial separation by geography. In many cases, one can also see huge quality of life differences that accompany these separations: wealthy Whites and a minuscule percentage of Blacks and other minorities living in middle class to high end, wealthy subdivisions, and the masses of Blacks living in hand-to-mouth poverty on the "other side of the tracks," mostly in inner cities. To illustrate, let us examine the city of Dallas, Texas, as a relevant example of ongoing segregation in housing. We will later see how segregated housing affects schools.

Iconic Dallas, Texas
From its nineteenth century agrarian origins until the twentieth century transformation to industrialization, Dallas, Texas was a city on an upward economic spiral. This trajectory was confirmed by a number of significant events, including a combination of the discovery of oil in the region and a construction boom in 1930; its position as a Mecca of high technology advancement and manufacturing in the latter half of the century; a rapidly growing real estate market; and visionary leadership. In synergetic fashion, this sequence of events spawned Dallas as a world class metropolis (www.dallashistory.org).

In 1985, I had occasion to travel to a four-day workshop in Dallas. The training sessions were held on the outskirts of the city near Addison, Texas, where my hotel was located. That was the first time I had been to Dallas and I seized the opportunity provided by the free time surrounding the sessions to randomly drive around several of the neighborhoods and sections that constitute that city. The experience was enlightening and gave me an interest-piquing first glimpse of the social and economic disparities that Dallas embodied. In Addison, I observed fine, well-appointed single family homes with Mercedes Benzes and an occasional Rolls Royce parked in the driveways. In South Dallas, I saw run-down, neglected homes, boarded-up houses, and dirt roads. It was the first time in my forty years of travel that I had seen dirt roads in the heart of a major city that was paved elsewhere.

Dallas, Texas is the ninth largest city in the United States and the third largest in Texas. Covering a sprawling 384.7 square miles, it is the essence of a metropolitan area due east of and including Forth Worth, Texas. The 2000 census attributed a total population of 1,188,580 to Dallas. The city's website boldly and proudly proclaims the city as among the 100 most ethnically diverse communities in the United States (www.dallascityhall.com). But this statement belies the distribution of the various populations.

In terms of religious presence, Dallas, a Bible Belt city, is home to large populations of Protestants, Catholics, Mormons, Jews, Eastern Orthodox Christians, Jesuits, Muslims, and Buddhists. The 2007 census estimates indicate the city's major ethnic make up to be 56.9% White and 23.8% Black. While Dallas historically has been predominantly White, it will be shown below that various race-related events of the twentieth century have produced sizable intra-city demographic shifts (factfinder.census.gov).

In the two decades from the years leading to the Great Depression to the end of World War II, America experienced population shifts of a magnitude rarely seen before or since. Shrinking regional job markets and resultant financial desperation forced whole families to uproot and strike out to those regions holding promise of employment. This dynamic led to a population explosion in commercially burgeoning Dallas that saw its number of inhabitants increase by 13.2% from 1930 to 1940 (Wilson, 1998).

At the same time, the city was experiencing growing pains of another kind as its Black population, which constituted 17.1% of the total, lived thoroughly segregated from Whites and shoe-horned into 3.5 square miles divided into six neighborhoods (Wilson, 1998). Discontent with overcrowded, squalid, crime-plagued living conditions, Black "Dallasites" sought to redress their plight by appealing to the town business elite for purchase of their own subdivision of affordable single family homes. This meant getting the approval of the Dallas Citizens' Council, the city's de facto government of the 1930s to 1950s (Phillips, 2006).

Despite their well-organized strategy and hat-in-hand demeanor (a given for 1940s southern Blacks seeking the favor of Whites), Black citizens of Dallas found no sympathetic ear. Negotiation after negotiation broke down as word of each proposed subdivision site reached nearby Whites, who professed fear of deflating property values and crime as reasons for opposition. Meanwhile, the ever increasing Black population swelled by an astounding 65.4% in metropolitan Dallas between 1940 and 1950 (Wilson, 1998).

Not all of the business elite of Dallas lacked sympathy for the plight of area Blacks. In 1948, Edward T. Dicker, of the Dallas Home Builders Association, proposed a subdivision that could house 30,000 Black "Dallasites" in a well-planned community of frame houses and apartment buildings. The proposal was resoundingly opposed, first via protest but soon followed by threats of legal action; this despite the fact that the subdivision would be four road miles from the nearest White community (Wilson, 1998).

Despite the obvious anxiety and longsuffering endured by Black citizens of 1950s Dallas, the White citizens of that city ultimately capitulated and the Hamilton Park subdivision was established in 1953. Hamilton Park represented victory for Blacks of Dallas. Within the decade, pioneering Blacks had withstood no less than a dozen bombings of homes they purchased in previously all-White sections of South Dallas. Whites ultimately conceded South Dallas to lower class Blacks. But Hamilton Park symbolized African Americans' economic propulsion to the middle class. This point is significant in exploring motives for segregation in that it renders class as a non-issue, leaving race starkly alone as the primary, underlying reason for White Dallas' desire for segregation.

Today, Dallas' penchant for Black-White separation has changed little in the years since the establishment of Hamilton Park. A breakdown of the 2000 census shows that Whites constituted 50.8% of the city's overall population and Blacks 25.9%. But as we examine subsections of the city, we find the affluent Park Cities area of Dallas, the collective name applied to the Town of Highland Park and the City of University Park, had a racial makeup of 95.14% White and 1.14% Black (www.factfinder.census.gov). Exclusive Preston Hollow epitomizes the trend, with its $40 million estates and $800,000 *tear-down* homes (at this writing, Preston Hollow is the new home of former President George W. Bush). The community didn't admit its first Black resident until 2000 (www.huffingtonpost.com), making it virtually all White. In sharp contrast, at the dawn of the new millennium, South Dallas was 33% Hispanic, 57% Black (www.bju.edu), and home to many of Dallas' marginalized working poor.

Atlanta, New York of the South

The history of Dallas' last century greatly parallels that of Atlanta, Georgia in terms of strained race relations and Black citizens' struggle for equity and equality in housing and life in general. From reconstruction to the late 1950s, Atlanta's Black citizenry lived under what Winston Grady-Willis calls petty and full apartheid (Grady-Willis, 2006), purposefully likening the city's policies and practices to the oppressive pre-1994 South African social structure. Data gathered by the Whitney Young-led Atlanta Committee for Cooperative Action documented vast differences between the lives of White and Black Atlantans. Regarding living accommodations, Blacks accounted for 35.7% of the city's population while living on 16.4% of the developed residential space. Not only did Blacks dwell in greater population density than Whites, their rented homes usually lacked the amenities, like private bathrooms and hot water that White citizens took for granted.

Like Dallas, Atlanta had experienced phenomenal economic prosperity in the early 20th century. Between 1900 and 1910, eleven major railroads had used the city as a center for distribution of goods due to its excellent east-west strategic location. Bank clearings more than doubled, totaling $96,000,000 in 1900 and more than $300,000,000 just ten years later; taxable property increased by nearly 20%; and manufacturing increased more than 60%. For the time period, Atlanta ranked second in the United States behind Los Angeles in proportional growth. This included the erection of more than 1,500 buildings between 1902 and 1906 (Bauerlein, 2001).

Amid Atlanta's burgeoning prosperity there existed a growing unrest among its Black inhabitants regarding strategies for breaking through the economic ceiling imposed by the city's post-reconstruction, Jim Crow-dominated social order. On the one hand, were Blacks who subscribed to Booker T. Washington's plan for overcoming through segregation, muted politics, and manual training in industrial skills. Washington's gradualist approach to economic emergence for Blacks sought to uplift the race by targeting the labor niche for their masses and not challenging Blacks' "place" in the Southern caste system. Per Mark Bauerlein (2001):

> "[White] Atlanta embraced [Washington] as Leader of His Race, a conservative theorist admitting his people's limitations and controlling their militant energies." (p. 107)

Diametrically opposed to Washington's plan was the radical, almost militant strategy of Atlanta's Black intellectual elite. Among them were Niagara Movement member and *Voice of the Negro* managing editor, J. Max Barber; Souls of Black Folk author and Niagara Movement leader, W.E.B. DuBois; convention organizer, William T. White; Bishop Henry M. Turner, Bishop of The African Methodist Episcopal Church in Atlanta, Black Nationalist and Back-to-Africa advocate; John Hope, President of Atlanta Baptist College (which later became Morehouse College); and other delegates of the 1906 Georgia Equal Rights Convention.

The various slates of the convention sought social equality and economic parity for Blacks through simultaneous attacks on the openly racist policies of the Georgia penal system, tax codes, emigration, and the vast array of measures designed by Whites to hamstring progress of Blacks (Bauerlein, 2001). Though Blacks disagreed about which strategy best addressed the problems of deplorable, overcrowded housing conditions and neo-slavery employment opportunities, all concurred that radical change was in order.

Early twentieth century Black Atlanta residents embodied the proverbial irresistible force, albeit peaceful, and segregationist Whites the immovable object. Racial tensions reached a crescendo following several years of Whites' fears of Black economic and social advancement accompanied by newspaper headline-stoked accounts of real and exaggerated sexual assaults by Black men on White women (1906atlantaraceriot.org). In early 1900s Atlanta, most such assaults, real or exaggerated, culminated in a public lynching. By the fall of 1906, Atlanta experienced a violent explosion not seen before or since that set the city's race relations tone for more than half a century.

On the evening of Saturday, September 22, 1906, the aforementioned conditions converged as a mob of half-drunk White men emptied into the streets from the city's just-closed Whites-only downtown bars. Before long the throng had swelled to 10,000 city and suburban Whites ranging from excitement-seeking onlookers to those hell bent on mayhem. As if on cue, the mob moved rapidly and purposefully through town toward the Black establishments and neighborhoods breaking windows, throwing bottles and bricks, chasing and beating to death any Blacks they encountered.

The situation got progressively worse in a hurry as the rioters happened upon several hardware stores and either purchased or looted firearms. Blacks in the path of the crush scurried for their lives. Those men and women captured were beaten, shot multiple times, mutilated, and hung out for public display. The riot – it has been called a riot but "massacre" is more appropriate as there was little retaliation by Blacks – lasted through the night and continued sporadically for several days with the crowd decreasing in size.

It was apparent early on during the insurrection that local police were vastly outmanned and outgunned. In one incident, rioters showed blatant disregard for their authority as they beat one Black man in plain view of one officer who clubbed his way through the assailants and pulled the badly injured man to safety. Local authorities were compelled to call upon Governor Joseph Terrell, who activated the state militia and threatened martial law. The mob action was finally quelled on September 24th by troops that were then stationed in the city. The final toll of perhaps the most shameful occurrence in Atlanta's history was 25 Blacks and 2 Whites dead with untold property damage (1906atlantaraceriot.org; Bauerlein, 2001).

As we fast forward through twentieth-century Atlanta to the 1960s, we find fascinating parallels and consistencies with the first decade of the century. In the context of race relations, the riot of 1906, its ensuing folklore, and opportunist, race-baiting White supremacist politicians served to hold White Atlantans in the grip of "negrophobia" (Bauerlein, 2001). Conversely, Black Atlantans held fast to mistrust of Whites, who they felt locked them in an economic and social time warp of White supremacy and Black subservience. Statistics served to support Blacks' wariness.

In reality, the Black Atlantan of the 1960s fared poorly in employment relative to his White counterpart. The overwhelming majority of African Americans were routinely shut out of all but the most menial jobs, leaving domestic and blue collar work as their likely options. Whites outnumbered Blacks nine to one as social workers; two-hundred to one as bookkeepers; twenty to one as electrical workers; and thirteen to one in general white collar employment. Only thirty-one Blacks were among Atlanta's eight-hundred policemen. Not a single Black attorney was employed by the city and the White-Black ratio of lawyers in the Fulton County solicitor general's office was 25 to 1. This occurred at a time when Blacks comprised greater than one-third of the city's population (Grady-Willis, 2006).

The decade of the 1960s was also similar to the first decade of the twentieth century: Atlanta existed as a tenuous racial powder keg. Progress had been made in an absolute sense, as Blacks were granted access to desegregated housing, public facilities, and accommodations such as libraries, buses, and golf courses. While the rest of the post-World War II South defiantly resisted desegregation, Atlanta appeared to embrace it. Of the racial tone of the city, Mayor William Hartsfield boasted that

"Atlanta is the city too busy to hate" (Kruse, 2005). But as in 1906, this seemingly idyllic peace was disrupted by a single incident that lit the fuse to the powder keg. In the aftermath, Atlanta was forever changed.

In America, harmony between Blacks and Whites precariously teeters at the precipice of discord or, worse yet, explosion. Despite its rhetorical proclamations, Atlanta, too, existed within this racial realm. The city that had successfully desegregated its schools in 1961 (Kruse, 2005) and tolerated White to Black neighborhood transformations was thrown into the throes of chaos triggered by the symbolism of a road barricade.

One year after Mayor Hartsfield's statement, city road crews erected a pair of road blocks in the subdivision known as Peyton Forest. On the face of it, the act seemed innocuous. But not coincidentally, the barricade was constructed at the exact dividing line between Black and White neighborhoods. Whites, feeling the encroachment of Blacks into turf that had historically been theirs, welcomed the partition. Blacks, who had broken ranks with the inner city to this middle class subdivision, took direct affront. The ensuing growing unrest caught the attention of the national and international press as some likened the barricade to the Berlin Wall and barriers encasing the Warsaw Ghetto (Kruse, 2005).

Blacks essentially fell into two camps on the issue: those who sought to address the problem in the courts and those advocating a more militant approach. While the former filed the necessary legal briefs, the latter, under the cover of night, burned the wooden barricades down. The following day, White road crews reconstructed the roadblock using steel instead of wood. For good measure, robed Klansmen served as sentries for several nights, patrolling the area with signs proclaiming their perceived right to live in segregated communities. In the end, the Black citizens prevailed as the courts ruled that the roadblocks were illegally constructed (Kruse, 2005).

For White Atlantans, the timing of the Peyton Forest incident could not have been worse. Black civil rights had been bolstered by the Brown Decision of 1954. In the political context, 1960s Atlanta was an epicenter of the American Civil Rights Movement, being the birthplace and headquarters of the Southern Christian Leadership Conference (SCLC), a focal point of The Student Nonviolent Coordinating Committee, (SNCC) and the home of Martin Luther King, Jr., Coretta Scott King; Ralph Abernathy; Joseph Lowery; and Andrew Young. In addition, The Atlanta University Center Consortium, the largest contiguous consortium of historically Black colleges and universities, was a hotbed of political activism and provided young, energetic manpower for the movement (www.georgiaencyclopedia.org).

Following the legal defeat of de facto segregation of Peyton Forrest and the affront presented by the barricades, Black realtors mounted an all-out effort to desegregate "Whites only" residential areas of the city. The resultant demographic shift was unlike anything previously witnessed. David Goldman, the character in British journalist Lynn Barber's coming-of-age novel, "An Education," perfectly summed up what followed in White Atlanta:

> "You want to know what stats are? Stats are old [White] ladies who are scared of colored people. So, we move the coloreds in and the old ladies move out. And I buy their flats cheap. That's what I do."

From 1957–1962, nearly 30,000 Whites had fled the city. During the 1960s, another 60,000 White Atlantans relinquished their homes to Black buyers. By the end of the 1970s, approximately 200,000 Whites left the city (Kruse, 2005). In perhaps the most dramatic example of White flight in American history, the city recorded African Americans as its majority population in 1972. In 2000, the Atlanta population of 416,474 was 33.2% White and 61.4% Black (quickfacts.census.gov).

The centuries-old, deep-rooted cultural belief in segregation of the races has firmly retained much of its historic fervor in the American South throughout the twentieth century. Thus one might expect that vestiges would remain today in cities like Dallas and Atlanta. Time has shown that racism, much like steel, is malleable. Whereas its original form may have been that of a sword, skillful hands with capable tools can morph it into the likeness of a dove. Nevertheless, the sword and the dove remain steel. And mitigated racism by any euphemism is still racism. While much of the South has overtly retained racial biases, political correctness has driven much of the North to more nebulous, subtle forms of racism.

Segregation in the North

Residential segregation accompanied by strained race-relations is not isolated solely in the American South. The sagas of Dallas and Atlanta have played out in countless northern cities as well. One could randomly select virtually any northern borough, town, township, or city and its adjacent suburban area and find neighborhoods, subdivisions, or sections that are de facto segregated by race. One prime example is my home town of New Brunswick, New Jersey.

Originally inhabited by the Lenape Indians, New Brunswick was chartered by Europeans in 1730 and incorporated 54 years later. Like Dallas and Atlanta, its rail and river waterway shipping access made it ideal for growth. This coupled with its location midway between New York City and Philadelphia made New Brunswick highly desirable for residence, business location, and university learning. Today the city is home to Johnson & Johnson's world headquarters; pharmaceutical giant Bristol-Myers Squibb; Rutgers-The State University of New Jersey; the University of Medicine and Dentistry of New Jersey, America's largest medical school; two premiere academic hospitals, three professional theaters, several four-star restaurants, and two four-star hotels. All this is found in a city of a mere 50,000 residents and only 5.8 square miles.

   Over the decades of the 1950's to the turn of the century, New Brunswick's residential racial divide has been fairly distinct. Robeson Village, a 58-unit public housing tract located in the Lincoln Gardens section of the city, consists of five streets lined with red brick two-story, multiple-unit, condo-type low income apartments. From its inception in 1946 to 2009, "the projects," as it is known, has been virtually all Black. In 1952, the subdivision added 200 units, with the new apartments known as Schwartz Homes. The miniscule number of White families whose income qualified them for residence in these projects were placed in Schwartz Homes.

   In the above time frame, Lincoln Gardens apartments, the White counterpart to Robeson Village/Schwartz Homes, was located about a half mile down Route 27 going toward the heart of the city. The two-story brick housing units were nearly identical in design to Robeson Village. The difference was who lived in them. I know of no Black families that lived in Lincoln Gardens Apartments at that time.

   Traveling another mile or so on Route 27, the main roadway through the city, one found more of the same. To the west, as one entered the city, were the homes of Hungarian immigrants and their families. During the half-century from 1950 to 2000, twenty-five percent of New Jersey's Hungarian community lived in New Brunswick. Strongly-rooted symbols of Hungarian culture remain in the city today. These include the Magyar Reformed Church and substantial business holdings like Magyar Savings Bank and Magyar Bancorp.

During the above period, most of New Brunswick's middle class African Americans resided in single family homes east of Route 27. Those who had purchased homes were part of integrated neighborhoods between Route 27 and Livingston Avenue, to the east, but most Black homeowners were concentrated in a roughly 34 square-block area east of Livingston Avenue approaching the E.R. Squibb factory. However, the highest density of poor Blacks could be found living in the Memorial Parkway Homes or public housing units south of the Raritan River and Route 18. This subsection and Robeson Village housed the vast majority of New Brunswick's poor Black population.

Today, the crime-ridden Memorial Parkway Homes as well as several blocks of lower class single family homes and apartments to the west are a not-too-distant memory, having gone by way of the wrecking ball in the last decade. For several years, the city's plans for purging poor Black "problem" elements via urban gentrification had been rumored. Concomitant with that rumor was the legal, ethical, and political dilemma of what to do with the thousands of displaced poor Black residents that were partly the object of the plan. Neighboring towns of Highland Park and Franklin Township had their own concentrations of Blacks. There were no plans to increase their numbers at the lower socioeconomic level.

When all was said and done, New Brunswick underwent total transformation of its downtown region, replacing blighted lower class housing with condominiums and townhouses, upscale businesses and restaurants, million-dollar penthouse apartments, and a multimillion dollar reconstruction of Route 18 and area roads. The end demographic result was that New Brunswick's Black population shifted from 29.6% in 1990, to 23.0% in 2000, then, to 14.1% in 2008.

While few would know the demographic history of small towns like New Brunswick, New Jersey, the media made millions aware of the issue of race in the planned community known as Levittown, Pennsylvania. The brainchild of building icon, William Levitt, Levittown placed the American dream of homeownership within financial reach of anyone who had the $8,000 asking price: that is, anyone who was White.

Levittown is one of several similarly-named northeastern subdivisions of affordably-priced, bare bones, cookie cutter single family homes built in the 1950s to meet the vast housing demands of post-World War II servicemen. These are the same men who fought in the European Theater of Operations, where they were part of racially-segregated infantry divisions, segregated living barracks, segregated mess halls, and segregated work assignments. Of these conditions, Stephen E. Ambrose writes in his books, *Citizen Soldiers: The U.S. Army from The Normandy Beaches, to the Bulge, to the Surrender of Germany*:

> "Old Jim Crow ruled in the Army as much as in the South. Blacks had their own units, mess halls, barracks, [and] bars--State-side, England, France, Belgium, it didn't matter."

It logically followed that returning White service men felt entitled to the privilege of living in White-only neighborhoods in the North as well as the South.

It is important to periodically reiterate throughout these pages that in no way do I believe that all White Americans subscribed to racial segregation or other forms of discrimination. Many Whites espoused true egalitarian American spirit and risked life, limb, and social standing to support the right of Blacks to purchase homes as their financial standing allowed. Levittown residents Bea and Lew Wechsler, Jewish political activists, were among those that took such a stand.

To be sure, there were negative social elements in the areas where large concentrations of Blacks were essentially compelled to live. As happened in Atlanta, Dallas, and numerous northern cities, high crime and poor schools were common. However, Blacks, unlike Whites, endured pressures to refrain from seeking out homes in towns like Levittown, where crime was virtually nonexistent and the schools were good. Just as Blacks in Dallas and Atlanta had done, many in the north took emotional and safety risks to realize the American dream of homeownership. When the Wechslers' neighbors put their house on the market in 1957, they presented Williams and Daisy Myers, African Americans, with their opportunity to live that dream. It would not be without its challenges.

The Myers' purchase of a home in Levittown was met with resistance like few Americans could endure. The sometimes violent protests were organized by the Levittown Betterment Committee, which included as many as 1,200 members. Their strategy employed constant noise directed at the Myers' home from a neighboring home purchased for that purpose and a cross burning by the Ku Klux Klan. That they held fast is a testament to their courage and strength of purpose as local police offered passive "protection," forcing the Myers' and their children to endure the harshest of harassment and dehumanizing treatment from their neighbors.

Willingboro, New Jersey and *the White Flight Phenomenon*

Whites' compulsion to segregate from Blacks in residential areas has been far from isolated occurrences in the North as well as the South. This trend, this social phenomenon, has repeated itself time and again throughout the United States. In 1950, South Dallas was a segregated community of Blacks and Whites with Blacks begrudgingly crowded into nine densely populated sections. When the housing dilemma reached crisis proportions in those Black sections, the residents responded by purchasing often overpriced homes in several of the formerly all-White areas. White residents expressed discontent in a variety of ways, first threateningly directing their protest at real estate agents and ominously driving in caravans through the target areas. When that proved fruitless, they turned the strategic clock back several decades and began bombing homes of new Black residents with some regularity (Grady-Willis, 2006).

The tactic understandably had a chilling effect on some Blacks but the entire set of circumstances affected Whites as well. Other Blacks found themselves between the rock of crushing overpopulation in the Black subsections and the hard place of violence-laced White protest. In the end, the situation gave rise to a stampede of White flight. In the 1950 U.S. census, 22,281 residents of South Dallas were White. Only 1,781 remained by 1960 (p.62). Thus, South Dallas was rapidly transitioned to the city's Blacks.

Willingboro, New Jersey is fifteen hundred miles north of Dallas and at least as far away culturally. Yet their approaches to separation of White from Black were strikingly similar and determined. Begun in the 1950s as yet another Levitt and Sons development, Wellingborough, as it was originally chartered, was to be the third and largest development of the Levitt organization. The project was known as Levittown New Jersey but confusion with its sister town twelve miles away in Pennsylvania led to its name being changed to Willingboro in 1959.

Though history portrays William Levitt as a visionary entrepreneurial American businessman who occupied an important social niche at a critical time in our country's history, Levitt was at the same time a social architect who possessed the means and will to hold racial progress at bay, albeit temporarily. In this newest and grandest of his subdivisions called Willingboro, Levitt's plan was to replicate the racial policies of his previous developments and build a utopian community with homogeneous values, religion, beliefs, ethnicity and living standards. Willingboro was depicted as representative of the American Way of Life.

Like its predecessor, Levittown, Pennsylvania, Willingboro remained all White until Blacks once again took to the American courts for the right to purchase homes there. It is ironic that Levitt's vision was to provide affordable single family homes to soldiers returning to America from World War II. However, W.R. James, an African-American officer stationed at nearby Fort Dix, was denied the opportunity to purchase a home in the subdivision based on his race. Even as James won the right to purchase in a lower court decision, Willingboro's "no Blacks" policy remained steadfast. It was not until the New Jersey Supreme court reinforced the lower court decision that James was allowed to live in Willingboro.

American history has taught us that Blacks' entrée into previously all-White neighborhoods is a predictor of cascading ethnic shift. Willingboro proved to be no exception. Despite efforts to stem the flow of Whites from the community by prohibition of "for sale" signs and other illegal or questionable means, the town rapidly shifted from all White to majority Black. In 1960, Willingboro's population of nearly 35,000 was all

White. By 2006, the town was 65.5% Black and 22.2% White. Once again, White flight had changed the face of an American community; not in the South, as one would expect, but in a very much northern setting.

The story of demographic shift in residential areas is a study in America's disingenuous and conflicted melting pot ideal. From the country's inception to the present day, European immigrants have been integrated into the mainstream and welcomed commensurate with their individual abilities to contribute to a particular American niche. Henry Kissinger, Albert Einstein, Arnold Schwarzenegger, Werner Von Braun, and Edward Teller are just a few prominent names on the nearly endless list of European Americans who achieved icon status and the freedom to use the substantial resources of the United States. African Americans, historically immiscible in that melting pot, have rarely been accorded the embrace received by their European-American brethren.

As symbols of White flight go, the racial evolution of Dallas, Texas pales in comparison to that of Atlanta, Georgia. Though spelled out previously, it bears repeating that the introduction of Blacks into previously all-White neighborhoods precipitated White emigration from urban Atlanta on a scale not seen before or since in any other American city. The legal defeat of de facto segregation of Peyton Forrest and other block-busting sections of the city gave the checkered flag to Black realtors to desegregate "Whites only" residential areas of the city. When the dust settled, nearly 30,000 Whites had fled the city by the early 1960s. Another 60,000 White Atlantans fled during the 1960s. Prior to 1980, 200,000 Whites left (Kruse, 2005). At the onset of the new millennium, Atlanta was 61.4% Black and 33.2% White.

CHAPTER THREE:
ADULTS, SCHOOL GOVERNANCE, AND THE GAP

> Let's say if they don't do well on the test...who should we blame for that... I believe that the school can make the difference, and so that's where I would look for the responsibility. This does not say that the community, the parents, the children...don't have some responsibility there. But I think the school is the organization that has to cause all of these other things to happen.
> -Rod Paige, Former Secretary of Education (pbs.org/frontline)

The Myth as a Concept

African American children have increasingly become the primary scapegoats for the failure of American education. In a system where there is more than enough blame to go around for the long-standing poor academic attainment and achievement test performance of urban and suburban schools, the fact that students' test scores have been deemed the primary indicator of academic success or failure singles out students as the causes of the system's bankruptcy.

The rationale for this statement is simple: students are the only stakeholders held accountable (through tests); the only ones with personalized files that document poor performance related to academics; and the only ones shouldering the personal shame and focused public scrutiny of failure. And while recent years have seen a marked uptick in cries for teacher and administrator accountability, the overwhelming majority of adults who govern and operate our schools fly under the radar of visibility and accountability. Such imbalance unfairly stigmatizes African American students by spotlighting shabby test performance. This shift of emphasis to the learner blames the victim, creating a smoke screen that helps to form the myth of the inept Black learner.

The Black-White achievement gap has been thrust upon the American public as some intractable problem that has withstood decades of concerted effort supported by billions of government dollars only to remain as entrenched as ever. To many Americans and foreigners alike, it is yet another extension of the centuries old "Black problem," the inescapable dilemma of what to do with and how to deal with America's slavery remnant. But as one researches carefully the adult public school stakeholders – federal and state education department hierarchies, local school boards, administrators, curriculum and instruction leaders, and teachers - one finds groups of adults whose cumulative sometimes cavalier or negligent acts, attitudes, and self-serving focus spawn achievement deficits that become manifest at test time. In reality, the Black-White achievement gap is a myth that should be more accurately called the "Systemic Efficacy Gap" between Black and White schools. Stated otherwise, the term "Black-White achievement gap" misrepresents the truth, misidentifies primary causal factors, and shifts focus from real solutions to victimized Black children.

Many Americans of all races privately embrace the delusion that Blacks lack intellectual essentials and that Black children are innately less predisposed to academic success than White children. In this regard, little has changed in the more than 200 years since Thomas Jefferson made the revealing quote cited on pages 36-37. But the coercion of political correctness demands that few but the most recalcitrant bigots will admit this publically. Moreover, teachers, administrators, and board members alike have long mitigated their failure to attack the gap and its companion (frustration) by placing Black children's academic failures firmly at the feet of dysfunctional Black parents and the purported inherent deficits of poverty and "Black culture" in general.

While poverty and poor parenting most certainly are correlates of academic underachievement, the achievement gap is an outgrowth of multiple factors that are not insurmountable if subjected to intelligent educational policies and sustained implementation of sound programs. Too often promising new programs that fail to show immediate results are killed and replaced as administrators and boards succumb to local political pressures to yield immediate success.

Policy structures in American public education are often well thought out, backed by sound science, and effectively piloted. But, when we consider overall broad scale student outcomes, it is clear (to date) that nothing has proven effective in enabling the masses of Black children to catch up. This criticism applies to The Elementary and Secondary Education Act of 2001, commonly known as No Child Left Behind.

No Child Left Behind

As an educational reform, The Elementary and Secondary Education Act of 2001, aka No Child Left Behind, appeared to show great promise and commitment to fair educational opportunity for all children, regardless of race. Simply stated, it held that by the year 2014, *all* racial, economic, and academic classification subgroups who attend public schools receiving Title 1 funds will be able to function on grade level in reading and mathematics. While other federal initiatives had fairly strong goals, NCLB was the first federal education initiative with accountability and transparency as its linchpins. In addressing the shortcomings of public education, particularly in urban schools, the newly elected President George W. Bush said in 2001:

> "Both parties have been talking about education for quite a while. It's time to come together to get it done, so that we can truthfully say in America: No child will be left behind."

Clearly he wasn't implying that wealthy, predominantly White schools, and their structural shortfalls had left their students behind. For NCLB was the most recent reform in a trail of education reforms that could be traced back to post *Brown Decision* initiatives and the decline of poor, urban, and urban rim education. Thus the Elementary and Secondary Education Act of 2001 was ushered in as the panacea for narrowing and closing the achievement gap or chasm separating Black and White test scores.

NCLB was a breath of fresh air to proponents of the right of all children to a "thorough and efficient education," as the New Jersey Constitution guarantees. Prior to its inception, educational reforms aimed at remediation of Black underachievement presented lofty achievement goals with toothless oversight and scrutiny of schools and districts with virtually no accountability. (At this writing, teachers were the only adult stakeholders facing serious accountability measures). As a result, all student achievement reporting was non-specific in terms of student racial and economic subgroups. Test scores were aggregated, allowing Black and poor students' underachievement to be hidden from public view in average score data. But, No Child Left Behind's disaggregation requirement laid bare the past sins of neglecting the children of color, special education students, and those living in poverty by placing these subgroups under the microscope.

When the NCLB clock began ticking in the year 2000, I was in my first year as principal of a small, mostly Black and Hispanic 400-student middle school in central New Jersey with abysmal test scores, a history of racial problems, and a huge achievement gap: only 14.6% of Black students passed the state test compared to 76% of Whites. I had witnessed the post *Brown-Decision* resistance to educational equality for African American children and welcomed a reform that finally appeared to have teeth, accountability, and transparency. But as the realities of enacting NCLB's high-bar standards set in, I vividly recall the contradictions in the program's initial foundation.

Prior to 2001, the initial accountability year, schools were required to examine all teaching staff and measure their credentials against a list of qualifying factors, including college credit hours earned in areas of certification and professional development pursuits. Each category was part of a point system and teachers were required to accumulate a certain number of points in order to attain the designation of "highly qualified" by the 2005-2006 school year. Those who failed to do so risked loss of employment thereafter.

In addition to qualifications of teaching staff, NCLB evaluated schools using up to forty-one quality "indicators." The number of quality indicators varied according to a school's grade span (elementary, middle, or high school). High schools had the highest number of indicators due to elements like graduation rate that would be absent at the elementary and middle levels. These indicators carried numerical standards that schools are required to meet in order to avoid the government's progressively punitive sanctions.

Said indicators addressed schools' outcomes not only in measures of achievement but also in areas of graduation rate, parental involvement, and student attendance. The greatest number of standards was in academic achievement with great emphasis on language arts literacy and math. In turn, progress in academic achievement was evaluated for individual student subgroups according to economic status, learning classification, primary spoken language, gender, and race.

The NCLB Startup Conundrum

As mentioned above, No Child Left Behind was unlike any other federal education mandate in terms of promise as well as tone. Its clear timelines for narrowing the achievement gap and the ominous nature of its set of successive sanctions for noncompliance made it controversial among polar constituents and placed it instantly at odds with the various state educational establishments. While some who had long awaited the fruit of the *Brown Decision* echoed a resounding "alas," states and Local Education Agencies (LEA's) viewed it as yet another of Washington's "unfunded mandates." But the threat of loss of federal funding compelled states and districts to comply begrudgingly with the letter of NCLB's tenets and timelines.

As with any new bureaucracy, No Child Left Behind encountered problems from its very onset. The states and LEA's each had well-established teaching forces aligned with the curriculum and instruction standards set by the fifty respective state credentialing departments. Moreover, state colleges and universities had largely trained new teachers in accordance with these criteria. On a national level, this created an incongruous, liberal hodgepodge of teacher quality that existed even as federal Department of Education thinking envisioned a model that would progress toward greater national unity in this regard. What it created was a conundrum of opposing forces that required Washington to make a decision if the initiative were to move forward.

To address the issue, NCLB established the "highly qualified" teacher designation that took into consideration the many thousands of entrenched teachers and their mishmash of credentials and preparation that deemed them suitable for service and capable in the classroom. While I have no statistics regarding the percentage of teachers who were relieved of their duties nationally for failure to attain the highly qualified status within the five year timeframe, I feel safe in saying that the number is miniscule based on my own experience as a principal overseeing the early stages of NCLB.

In the final analysis, the federal government, through the Department of Education, took either a tremendous leap of faith or the politically expedient way out in accepting the national teacher work force of 2001-2005. I'm inclined to lean toward the latter given the practicality of the situation as well as the huge political power brandished by the several national teacher unions.

From its first step of ordaining a fit national teaching force, No Child Left Behind was doomed for at least short term failure in terms of its achievement goals. After all, the national teacher force that existed in 2001 were virtually the very same people that had never been able to eradicate the huge test score gap between Blacks/Hispanics and Whites/Asians in years prior. Thus, there was little to give anyone strong hope that this same group of people could and would miraculously be transformed into so many master teachers capable of reaching the millions of poor and minority children that had previously fallen by the academic proficiency wayside.

Another point that may have thrown lay parents and NCLB reform watchers off stride is the very use of the thinly veiled rhetorical term "highly qualified" to describe America's teaching force. By contrast, as we view the nomenclature set aside for describing students achievement test outcomes we see words like "partially proficient" to describe a student's failure to meet the minimum New Jersey standard. Oddly, many of the teachers that were suddenly swept into the "highly qualified" realm had failed by any standard to teach enough of their subject matter to their students to attain class averages that were above that minimum standard.

In the final analysis, the United States Department of Education colluded with state education departments to give the public "highly qualified" status to teachers whose classes had failed to meet the minimum test score standard. This presented an obvious paradox that has not gone away after more than ten years of NCLB. Evidence of this fact is that to date, there are huge numbers of urban and suburban schools languishing at NCLB's "in need of improvement" status or worse.

Table 4 below provides a graphic depiction of the "highly qualified" teacher/failing student paradox as played out in eight randomly selected New Jersey schools representing a broad range of district factor groups. District Factor Groups (DFG's) are a range of designations for New Jersey schools based on a set of demographic factors that historically were deemed to impact student achievement. Those factors include family income, educational attainment of adults, and occupation. Averages for these factors are taken within the geographic confines of districts and each district is accordingly placed in a category ranging from A, for the poorest (urban) districts to J, for the wealthiest. Cities like Newark, Jersey City, Camden, and Trenton fall into DFG "A." Alpine Borough, Franklin Lakes Borough, and Upper Saddle River are examples of DFG "J" school districts.

TABLE 4:
Random Sample of NJ Schools with 100% Highly Qualified Teachers Compared to Percent <u>Failing</u> Test Scores for Black and White Students on 2010 NJASK 4

School	District	DFG	% HQ	White LAL	White Math	Black LAL	Black Math
New Jersey Ave. Ele.	Atlantic City	A	100	n/a	n/a	61.5	35.9
Cramer Ele.	Camden	A	96.2	n/a	n/a	89.2	83.8
Maude M. Wilkins Ele.	Maple Shade	CD	100	39.7	21.5	58.8	29.4
Bartle School	Highland Park	GH	100	19.6	8.9	46.7	46.7
Bradford Ele.	Montclair	GH	100	15.6	8.9	51.7	37.9
Ethel McKnight Ele.	East Windsor Reg.	GH	100	23.3	16.4	57.1	57.1
Lawrence Intermediate	Lawrence Townshp	I	100	29.1	18.5	71.4	54.8
George E. Wilson Ele.	Hamiltn Townshp	FG	100	50.0	62.5	70.8	50.0

65

The table illustrates that throughout the state of New Jersey, statistically significant percentages of students are walking out of schools at the end of each test year having been taught relatively little reading (LAL) and math by NCLB standards even though their teachers have been endorsed as "highly qualified." To the layman, this implies an exercise in deductive reasoning: if teachers in the above schools have the necessary expertise to teach and the students are failing, the deficiency likely falls upon the student.

These assumptions strongly imply that school personnel have done their parts but failing students cannot, for whatever reason, absorb what has been taught. Moreover, since urban and suburban Black students fail state tests disproportionately more than White students, the underachieving student now has a face, and it is Black. But, as we will see in succeeding pages, in the cases of failing classrooms, these assumptions are far from the truth. All teachers are not highly qualified experts in their subjects; the curricula are not always adequately covered; and the Black student does not and should not personify failure.

To the many who are witting or unwitting adherents to the achievement gap fallacy, the failure to learn falls upon the student. It is for these individuals that I have slowly and fairly laboriously in the previous pages built upon the premise that African American school children have been unjustifiably cast into a racist American social system that first isolates them residentially from White children as a prelude to similar physical, social, psychological, and emotional isolation in virtually all other facets of life in America. It logically follows that this separation would follow the Black child into the schoolhouse and its public school classroom.

While this segregation is quite noticeable in cities and their schools, where White students are in the extreme minority, it is less apparent to the unwary eye but just as real in suburban schools. The compulsion to separate Black and White students in suburban schools is sometimes subtle but very real. As we progress herein, we will examine some of the myriad ways adults set the stage for the Black-White achievement gap and orchestrate its existence by separating Black and White inside school walls.

Public Education as a Profession

The education model in America is an interesting contradiction when compared to other professions and when one considers the client-practitioner relationship. In all professions, the practitioner presumably provides a level of expertise sufficient to solving problems of or meeting the needs of the client. In most cases, the client's needs are weighed by the professional in light of one or more protocols which are then presented to the client for consideration. The two may collaborate and the client then chooses the path that is optimal to his or her benefit. This model plays out with regularity in law, medicine, accounting, and finance, to name a few.

The differences between the aforementioned professions and the practice of education are unlike the others. The educator's clients are all powerless children with virtually no voice in how the treatment is devised or delivered. To illustrate this point, let us consider a medical analogy in which an adult, after weight gain, notices a set of symptoms that include drowsiness after meals, increased thirst, and occasional blurred vision. Given these symptoms, a competent medical doctor might suspect the onset of type II diabetes. But he would not proceed with treatment or prescribe medication without running tests that can confirm or reject his hypothesis. Even after tests confirm that the initial diagnosis is correct and a diabetes protocol is in order, the medical client, being more than an equal partner in the doctor-patient relationship, may accept or reject the proposed treatment in favor of an alternative: a regimen of diet, exercise, and weight loss, for example.

Unlike the medical patient, the children (clients) in America's schoolrooms have few or no treatment options. From pre-k to grade 12, they are compelled to attend the schools in their city or town and to accept the "treatment" that is devised by the teachers and administration of the district and approved by the board of education. If these children are blessed to live in a wealthy community or attend private schools, it is likely they attend good schools run by competent professionals and this scenario is a benevolent one in which the "treatment" is near cutting edge and proven academically effective as determined by multiple measures that include achievement test scores. Wealthy children receive the kind of education that in all probability will advance their lives and optimize their life chances.

While no credible research identifies innate differences between suburban or urban Black and wealthy White children in terms of academic potential, student outcomes of large-city schools consistently differ markedly from those of wealthy schools as do test scores. The average African American urban student's life chances are greatly diminished and his test scores are among the poorest in the country. If they live in a suburban community near those cities, there is a high probability that they will receive an education that is substandard relative to what is received in a wealthy community.

But regardless of which socio-economic status (SES) levels of schools the African American child attends, research demonstrates that his test scores will be below those received by his White age group peers or classmates. To search for plausible explanations to this long-standing dilemma, we will delve into the contrasting actions of adults in urban and suburban schools with significant numbers of Black students versus those who govern, administer, and teach in wealthy, predominantly White suburban schools.

If one analyzes professional/client relationships in general, it becomes clear that the balance of benefits usually is tipped considerably to the side of the client. Certainly doctors and lawyers benefit greatly in many ways from their practices but their foci are necessarily on their clients because they are accountable to them by oath and professional ethics. They depend on clients for their livelihoods. Unhappy clients in this day of instant mass communication via Twitter or Facebook can wreak havoc on a lawyer's practice over time. But this balance of client-professional benefit, focus, and accountability has somehow, somewhere fallen by the wayside in education to a point where emphasis has shifted to the wants and needs of adult stakeholders – board members, teachers, administrators - often to the detriment of children.

Boards of Education

Present day school boards are modeled after those begun over 200 years ago in colonial Massachusetts. As the early colonies grew in population and complexity, governance of public schools necessarily shifted from being within the direct purview of states to being under the operation of local boards within the jurisdictional parameters established by the states (Danzberger, J.P. et al, 1992).

Through the nineteenth century, urban boards of education were typically comprised of elected representatives of the various city sectors or wards. This fact underscores the long-standing political nature of boards of education throughout the eastern states and on westward as the country grew. To the present day, local boards of education are usually elected by the voters but may also be appointed by elected officials (Hess, Frederick M., 2002).

By the late 1800s, the public nature of schooling and its governance placed urban public schools and their boards in a position of visibility and constant critique, due in large part to the growing diversity of neighborhoods and struggles for equity among the various populations. These and other concerns gave rise to reforms of the board of education model spearheaded by elite professionals, businessmen, and educators. The resulting changes brought about a bifurcation of the roles of school boards and superintendents toward a business model wherein boards developed and established policy and superintendents acted as CEOs in district administration (Danzberger, 1992).

American boards of education had existed in increasing numbers over the years with relatively minor variations in structure and autonomy. All of that changed in fairly rapid fashion in the last half of the twentieth century on the heels of two major events: the Brown v. Board of Education of Topeka, Kansas Supreme Court decision and the launching of Sputnik by the Soviet Union. Though both events decreased the policymaking autonomy enjoyed by boards by compelling them to adhere to state and federal edicts, in the context of our focus, the Black-White achievement gap, it is the Brown decision that attracted most of the attention of boards and their constituents from Maine to California. Post Brown, American school districts could no longer operate under the separate-but-equal doctrine and give Black children short shrift in the myriad ways it was doled out since the 1896 Plessy decision.

It is noteworthy to point out that while the various petitions that collectively constitute the Brown case were originally filed against districts below the Mason-Dixon line, in many cases Northern schools were nearly as segregated as those in the South. But in the North, segregation was de facto under the guise of "neighborhood schools." Nevertheless, the result was the same in the North and the South: Black children and White children were divided in schooling just as they were residentially.

The Brown decision in one fell swoop changed all this by requiring that integration trump the convenience of neighborhood schools or the preference of parents for racial separation. Thus, from the early 1970s through the early 1990s, race-related issues like bussing and school program equity occupied space on school board agendas and became a very large part of their political concerns.

The Role of Boards

Regardless of whether a particular board of education is elected or appointed, all are charged with writing, adopting, and establishing the policies and regulations that guide every program and action of the districts over which they preside. From this standpoint, one must rightly conclude that the achievement gap begins at the meeting table of boards of education as they are responsible for the academic substance and social tone of a district. Moreover, as extensions of the taxpayers of their respective municipalities, they are the internal eyes, ears, and conscience of district parents, legally charged with protecting children in the myriad ways schools affect them.

Virtually nothing of significance can and should take place that has not been approved or sanctioned by the board of education. Curriculum, extracurricular activities, hiring, staffing levels, staffing diversity, and instructional philosophy are examples of major areas controlled and endorsed by the board of education under the advice and guidance of the administrative hierarchy and faculty. Thus, the responsibility for adopting policies that attack racial inequity and promote fairness in schools begins, from a program policy standpoint, with the local board of education.

A Psychology of Separation

In Chapter 2, we addressed America's long-standing penchant for racial separation in residential areas. A subtle psychological tone is set as it is common for distinct residential areas to display ethnic names and to have defined roadway, natural, or physical boundaries, e.g. railroad tracks. Nineteen-eighties Chicago may have been the poster city for this unwritten rule. Throughout the city, anyone could see distinct ethnic divisions identified by ethnic-language signs that staked out neighborhoods. It was as if little to no effort was made toward amalgamation, whether by immigrants' preference or local obstacles to ethnic absorption into the White mainstream.

America has actually upheld abstract separation of the races via unwritten rules for nomenclature. One such rule requires municipal subdivisions, major landmarks or areas inhabited by Whites to have neutral, American, or European names. For example, the states of the East like New York and New Jersey, which were part of the original colonies, have a plethora of towns named for Jefferson, Washington, Hamilton, and Franklin. Even relatively new towns follow this pattern. Landmarks like the Verrazano-Narrows Bridge and the Pulaski Skyway are named for Europeans. Minor variations of the rule may involve using Native American names like Rancocas and Hopatcong.

Accordingly, Black-inhabited neighborhoods, buildings, and structures within these municipalities may have European or Black names. However, White areas are not named for Black Americans. Nor are major landmarks or buildings within White areas named for Blacks. One would be hard pressed to find a municipal subdivision, street, school or landmark in a historically and predominantly White residential area that is named after Martin Luther King, Harriet Tubman, Malcolm X. Shabazz, or other nationally-prominent Black American despite the deserved recognition of the individual for that honor. It follows that when one drives on Martin Luther King Boulevard or Malcolm X Shabazz Avenue in any number of American cities, one is fairly certain to be in a predominantly Black section of that city.

<u>School Boards, Policy, and the Will of the People</u>
    This point about racial division in the abstract and concrete is important within the context of local school boards given that school boards, whether elected or appointed, are political entities. As such, their membership is shaped not necessarily in accordance with population percentages but rather by the political forces within the municipality. And while Blacks may comprise a majority or significant minority population within a municipality, political power and White coalitions, formal or informal, within that municipality commonly skew board membership in favor of Whites, despite the size of the White population.
    Stark evidence of this fact can be found in a 2002 report published by the University of Virginia for the National School Boards Association. In a survey of the school boards of 2,000 of America's 14,890 school districts, membership on these boards was found to be 85.5% white, 7.8% African American, and 3.8% Hispanic. In large, mostly urban districts with more racially diverse populations, the ethnic breakdown of school board membership remained similar: 78.9% white, 13.0% African American, and 7.5% Hispanic (Hess, Frederick M, 2002). Thus, one may readily and accurately conclude that despite the

overwhelmingly minority racial composition of a large number of America's cities and towns, their school boards are often found to be either majority or significantly White in membership.

This demographic data alone makes no definitive statement about school board policymaking vis a vis race, racism, and/or the Black/White achievement gap. And such a misrepresentation would be a grave disservice to the thousands of dedicated school board members of all races who manifest egalitarian sentiment in their policymaking. However, when this demographic data is juxtaposed to racial breakdowns of student populations versus scholastic structures, one gets a clearer picture of the correlations of board membership to Black achievement and the achievement gap.

In years prior to the Brown decision, prior to political correctness, and before the push for social tolerance in American culture, only the most enlightened boards of education in racially diverse areas gave any consideration at all to matters of true, effective racial equity from a policy standpoint. In fact, the rule of the land was racial separation in residence and schooling; this signaled the need for intervention from the courts. Given this pervasive condition throughout the country, Brown actualized White parents' worst fears by requiring that schools be desegregated. This was especially true in the South, which had most vehemently resisted racial mixing. So, to accommodate the Brown decision, throughout the '70s and '80s, Black children were bussed to previously all-White or nearly all-White schools to meet the letter of the law.

Despite the "all deliberate speed" language in Brown, ordering rapid desegregation, the 1954 Brown decision was not the end-all to bring about racial parity in America. This fact was demonstrated by White resistance to desegregation and the subsequent need of advocates for Black children to again use the courts to pry public school equity from recalcitrant grips in the South as well as in the North.

One example of this point occurred on June 30, 1968, as the Edgewood Concerned Parent Association, representing their children and similarly situated students, filed suit in federal district court for the Western District of Texas against the San Antonio Independent School District et al (Rodriguez v. San Antonio Independent School District). The parents contended that Texas' use of a property tax-based system of school financing violated the equal protection clause of the Fourteenth Amendment to the U. S. Constitution. The case, which reached the U.S. Supreme Court in 1972, ended in defeat for the plaintiffs, with the High Court ruling that the Texas system of school finance did not violate Constitutional protections.

Just as the Rodriguez case was having a chilling effect on southern Black and Hispanic struggle for equal educational opportunity, similar cases were being played out in state courts, including New Jersey and California. In New Jersey, Robinson v. Cahill was a case filed on behalf of Kenneth Robinson, a gifted Jersey City 12 year old denied an appropriate education by New Jersey's property tax-based system of school finance. Similar to the San Antonio case, disparate property tax bases between wealthy and poor communities created great disparities in educational quality between those school districts.

The *Robinson* case evolved into Abbott v. Burke until 1985, when the Supreme Court of New Jersey eventually ruled in favor of the plaintiffs, declaring the state's funding system to be unconstitutional and requiring that per pupil spending be increased in poor urban districts to reach parity with wealthy districts to meet the state constitution's requirement of providing a "thorough and efficient" system of education. Despite this, in 2010, New Jersey Governor Chris Christie revised the urban funding formula downward, effectively reversing the Court's funding requirement.

In *Serrano v. Priest*, which spanned three California Supreme Court opinions between 1971 and 1977, similar school funding battles were fought. *Serrano* originated as a class action brought on behalf of a class of all California public-school pupils. The case epitomized the American struggle of haves vs. have-nots and the battle against racial discrimination. As happened in New Jersey, the Court's ruling on behalf of the plaintiffs struck down California's public-school financing structure as a violation of equal protection. Prior to the ruling, per-pupil expenditures varied greatly and depended on a school district's tax base, creating disparities that resulted in inequalities in actual educational expenditures per pupil (leagle.com/decision/1971).

The *Brown, Rodriguez, Abbott* and other similar suits brought between 1951 and 1985 represented monumental efforts to defeat codified and de facto segregation in American schools and to level the academic playing field for all children. But they failed to take into account America's seemingly ubiquitous resistance to racial equality and equity in public schools. The Black-White achievement gap and cavalier attitudes regarding its existence stand as looming testaments to this failure. Clearly placing Black and White children in the same schoolhouse only scratches the surface of what is needed to balance academic achievement among the races.

In American culture, it is a truism that the will of the powerful will eventually become manifest despite contrary laws or policies. Racial division in American schools is a classic example of this truism. The Brown decision forced White Americans out of a comfort zone of racial separation. As the Court demanded a push "with all deliberate speed" toward racial justice and equality in public education in the form of integration, public school districts throughout the nation began to follow the letter of the law. But the politically savvy continued to look for ways to fulfill the letter of the law while maintaining or regaining their former racially separate, Whites-on-top status. Having elected their advocates to local school boards, they soon realized that many tools were at their disposal that would allow them to emulate within schools the values of the greater society. In the following chapter, we will explore several of the major structures and strategies that presented themselves as paradoxical in proposed purpose and outcome.

CHAPTER 4:
RACIAL BIAS INSIDE THE SCHOOLHOUSE

> Ironically, even as the federal government has endorsed the principle of educational equity…it has done very little to address the unequitable conditions under which children learn. In fact, despite all of the attention to standards, no state government has adopted basic opportunity to learn standards, similar to standards for highways or utilities, for which it can be held accountable.
>
> -Dr. Pedro Noguera, *"School Reform and Second Generation Segregation."*

To this point, we have seen that what we know as the achievement gap fundamentally has its beginnings in and strongly correlates with the American cultural value for separation of the races in all major aspects of life, especially including public schools. Those who believe we now live in a post racial society will cite the successes of numerous African Americans including President Barack Obama, world renowned television superstar Oprah Winfrey, former Merrill Lynch CEO Stanley O'Neal, and many others, to name but a few. But from a relative standpoint these individuals are miniscule in number and great exceptions to the rule that confines and restricts success parameters for the masses of Blacks.

Confirmation of the fact that race plays a significant role in probability of Blacks' socioeconomic advancement in America lies in Bureau of Labor Statistics data on employment rates for Black and White Americans. Whereas data for September of 2011 found 7.2% of Whites to be unemployed, Black unemployment was more than double that rate at 15.9%. If we fast forward one year to September 2012 in this improving-but-still-difficult economic period, we find White unemployment declining to 6.3% and Blacks still more than doubled that rate at 13.4% unemployment (bls.gov/news.release/empsit.t02.htm). A review of BLS data for virtually any decade for the last century will uncover similar trends of disparity in Black and White opportunities for economic, and thus social, advancement in America. Given the strong correlation of income to educational attainment, public school quality, and academic achievement, one readily understands why African Americans' ongoing dismal employment trends foretell the dire need for improvement in educational opportunities in public school.

Despite America's collective denial of its race-conscious nature, the title of Dr. Andrew Hacker's 1992 book is still quite relevant as it succinctly describes the stark reality of the lives of Blacks in American culture: <u>Two Nations Black and White, Separate, Hostile, and Unequal</u>. These "two nations" provide the backdrop and social context for schools in our cities and towns. And the separation, hostility, and inequality meet our children at the schoolhouse door.

Law and Order in American Schools

Increasingly conservative approaches to crime and punishment in our greater society precede like themes and trends found in our schools. So it holds that just as arrests and incarceration rates affect African Americans in far greater proportions than European Americans relative to their percentages of United States populations, Black male and female students are vastly more likely to bear the severe brunt of office referrals, suspensions, and expulsions in schools throughout the country. This contributes to root causes of the achievement gap, for it logically follows that a student who is suspended out of school is deprived of the optimal learning environment. Upon returning to school he or she will in all probability lag behind his or her non-suspended classmates commensurate with time out of the classroom. That lag becomes palpable at test time as all enrolled students are compelled to sit for standardized tests.

Inasmuch as school policies embody the sentiments, values, and beliefs of their regional citizenry, one need look no further than the local and state communities to gain an understanding of the factors that influence discipline statistics. Put more succinctly, regional race relations and attitudes very strongly influence school discipline policies in a way that mirrors criminal justice trends.

According to a 2007 report published by the Sentencing Project, a national non-profit organization engaged in research and advocacy on criminal justice policy issues, the year 2005 found more than 2.2 million Americans behind bars, the highest incarceration rate in the world. Of that number, an alarming 900,000 (41%) were African American. According to Bureau of Justice Statistics data, one of every six Black American men had been incarcerated in 2001. It predicted that if the trend of imprisoning Black men continues, one of every three born in 2007 would be imprisoned in their lifetime (Bonczar, Thomas P., 2003). It is noted that the rate of imprisonment of Black women is considerably lower than that of men.

As much as we would like for our schools to provide a utopian protective shield for our children that fairly and justly blocks out society's ills, reality prevails such that aspects of all of the social elements present in American culture can be found in the halls, lunchrooms, and classrooms of public schools. So, just as laws exist to provide a sense of safety and law and order in greater American society policies, supporting regulations, and rules are in place in schools to control student behavior and discipline and provide a sense of safety and order. However, a view of discipline outcomes strongly suggests that children of color may be more often victimized than their white classmates by the policies, rules, and regulations that purportedly protect them.

According to published data from the U.S. Department of Education for the 2004-2005 school year, Black students in schools in 21 states were suspended at rates more than double their percentages in the student populations (nces.ed.gov/pubs2005). Those data found that in Minnesota Black students were suspended 6 times as often as Whites. In Iowa, where Blacks comprise only 5% of public school populations, they accounted for 22% of suspensions. In New Jersey public schools, African-American students were almost an astounding 60 times as likely as white students to be expelled for serious disciplinary infractions. These are the findings published in 2007 in a Chicago Tribune report on race and discipline by senior correspondent Howard Witt (articles.chicagotribune.com/2007-09-25/).

Blacks are not the only ethnic minorities affected by unequal incarceration trends. According to government data, imprisonment of Hispanics increased by 43% since 1990, with Spanish-speaking men comprising 20% of the state and federal prison populations in 2005. If the trend continues, 17% of Hispanic males born in 2007 can expect to go to prison in their lifetime.

But incarceration trends tend not to be mirrored in discipline rates for all racial groups in public schools. Whereas African Americans are disciplined at a higher rate than their population numbers, they stand alone among all ethnic groups in terms of this disparity. The federal data show that Hispanic students are suspended and expelled nearly in proportion to their populations, while white and Asian students are disciplined at rates far less than those of Blacks and Hispanics.

Educators who have worked extensively with Black children can cite incidents of untoward behavior by their charges. But according to Dr. Russell Skiba, a professor of educational psychology at Indiana University whose research focuses on race and discipline issues in public schools, Black students are no more likely to commit rules offenses than other students from similar social and economic environments. This strongly suggests that race is a major factor in the shaping of discipline policy and resultant punishment involving Black students.

It most certainly holds true that some lower SES Black children grow up in impoverished neighborhoods and come from single parent or absentee parent homes. These challenges frequently leave them less trained than their White classmates in middle class social norms and behavioral expectations in school. While these socioeconomic factors contribute to disproportionate discipline rates, researchers find that poverty alone cannot explain the disparities. According to Dr. Skiba:

> "In the absence of a plausible alternative hypothesis, it becomes likely that highly consistent statistical discrepancies in school punishment for black and white students indicate a systematic and prevalent bias in the practice of school discipline." (Skiba, Michael, Nardo, 2000)

Anecdotal Evidence: Prisons and Black Youth

Through the early 1970s, I had the good fortune to work with the Teacher Corps Corrections Project, a uniquely chartered federally-funded mission designed to impact recidivism among urban high school students. I first worked as an intern in Newark, New Jersey schools from 1972-1974, then as a team leader from

1974-1976, supervising teacher-interns placed in youth prisons and public schools.

During my stint as Team Leader, my weekly itinerary took me to several correctional institutions throughout the state of New Jersey, including Annandale Reformatory, Trenton State Prison, Bordentown Reformatory, and Jamesburg Youth Reformatory. Annandale Reformatory, now renamed Mountainview Youth Correctional Facility, is situated in rural Hunterdon County, New Jersey. Bucolic and devoid of bars, the facility looked more like a country retreat, or county college campus than a prison. On one of my many trips to Annandale, I happened upon an annual tradition, ritual if you will, in which New Jersey's criminal court judges donned their black robes and spent a good portion of the day walking the grounds and hallways interacting with and among the inmates. While their intent for this annual ritual was no doubt to impart something positive to all involved, their purpose was lost on me as I took in the stark fact that the judges were virtually all White and the inmates were nearly all Black.

Annandale's criminal court judges and Black youthful offenders are a small part and polar opposite ends of a vast American criminal justice system that somehow has gone awry; a system where Blacks, young boys and men in particular, are disproportionately profiled, surveilled, arrested, convicted, and incarcerated to a far greater extent and treated far more harshly than Whites in the United States. The climate that facilitates this phenomenon is the same dark cloud of bias that follows Black boys and girls to school each day; a bias that is deeply and surreptitiously embedded in school discipline codes.

Anecdotal Evidence: Black Youth and Discipline Trends

Nearly three decades after my Teacher Corps experience I entered my first year as vice principal/disciplinarian of a suburban middle school outside of Trenton, New Jersey. I was coming from seven years as science teacher in a majority Black middle class district and joined the administrative team in early July. The district afforded me the luxury of a month-long period of training under my African American predecessor, who was also a Baptist preacher and pastor.

After reviewing key aspects of the job and sharing insights gained in his 25 years at the school, my predecessor proceeded to share a firm warning with me: watch out for "Hot Dog." Keep him under your thumb. Hot Dog (not his real nickname) was a short, chunky Black boy who had more than his share of run-ins with the faculty and was at the top of everyone's hit list. I found it curious that of all the more than 1,300 students at the school, my predecessor saw fit to warn me about only one pudgy little Black boy.

Being a science and math person, I approached my new job scientifically and soon compiled discipline statistics by offense, grade level, interdisciplinary team, gender, and race. My purpose was not only to mete out discipline but also to use these data to devise preventative strategies for the long term via humanistic pupil control. Somewhere midyear, a fairly shocking pattern began to develop: even though Black students were only 40% of the student population, they comprised 90% of the office referrals. Astounded by these numbers, I took my findings to my weekly administrators' meeting with the principal (I was the only Black administrator) who in turn suggested that I bring the issue up for discussion at the next faculty meeting.

The office referral data begged several hypotheses from the standpoint of cause and effect. In nearly all student behavior cases that result in an office referral, there is some action by the student that is subjectively interpreted by the teacher as falling outside the scope of acceptability. So, one reasonable hypothesis was that the school had a troublesome batch of Black kids that acted out at a frequency disproportionate to their numbers. Another possibility was that Black students were being profiled by the majority White faculty. I soon received information that supported the latter hypothesis far more than the former.

American middle schools frequently schedule core subject teachers into interdisciplinary teams with each team member having the same prep time block. This format affords them the opportunity to utilize their common planning period for team meetings where problems are brainstormed and ideas shared. In my school, administrators often attended these meetings to get a feel for happenings in the building and to offer support to teachers. I was invited to one such meeting to offer my input on how to handle a problematic student that we will call "Sandy."

Sandy was an attractive, petite, bespectacled, feisty little White girl who, like Hotdog, had a less-than-ideal home life and a volatile personality. She lived with her financially struggling young single mother and two younger siblings. The mother worked as a bar-and-grill waitress and had a part time job in addition. The mother's brother was Sandy's father figure and occasional family disciplinarian given mom's difficulty in controlling her quick-tempered adolescent daughter.

In this particular team meeting, the consensus was that Sandy was on a prolonged string of acting-out incidents that culminated in her having a melt-down in the classroom in which she screamed at the top of her lungs at the teacher. The teacher simply let the child vent and took no action other than to speak with the child after class and place her on the team meeting agenda. I was mildly flabbergasted. Given that Hotdog was on the same team, my input to the teacher and the team, in light her lack of disciplinary action against Sandy was, "But you wouldn't take that from Hotdog!"

One could hear a pin drop in the classroom. I believe it was an epiphany for the teachers. Instantly they realized that in terms of student discipline, they had been living a double standard exemplified by these two children who had similar familial and behavioral backgrounds but who were racial polar opposites. The two children also demonstrated a bifurcation in the teachers' (and administration's) approaches to handling behavioral problems, approaches that were diametrically opposite and race-driven.

Anecdotal Evidence: White Teachers and Discipline Data

Stephen Sawchuk, assistant editor for Education Week specializing in teacher issues writes:

> "As the country's K-12 student population grows more ethnically diverse, students of color face the troubling possibility of never having a teacher who looks like them. According to federal data, more than 40 percent of students are nonwhite, compared to just 17 percent of teachers, and that mismatch appears to be on the rise." (edweek.org/ew/contributors/stephen.sawchuk.html)

This imbalance in backgrounds among teachers and students, and the fact that teachers and students often live apart in ethnically homogeneous neighborhoods, serve to perpetuate misunderstanding and ignorance, one about the other. I've had first-hand experience in this realm as an African American vice principal and principal in urban rim schools where the vast majority of faculty was white.

On the heels of the aforementioned administrators meeting, I placed my race-related office referral findings on the faculty meeting agenda for discussion and reflection among the nearly all-white faculty and administration. The insightful reader might predict the outcome. Though my presentation was carefully worded as a non-accusatory statement of fact, and though I emphasized that the statistics were only numbers that simply implied a problem worthy of investigation, my words were interpreted as finger-pointing by the faculty.

Guided by the self-same racial insensitivity that spawned the divide between them and their Black students, a surreptitious movement developed wherein my faculty colleagues opted to kill the messenger. My efforts to expose the elephant in the room and level the playing field for Black students were met with resentment. From that point on, my days at the school were numbered and I found myself riffed after my first year.

From the civil rights era days to the present, suburban schools with significant Black student populations of 30% or more have sought out appropriate individuals to serve as buffer between White and Black. The usual roles were often vice principal, guidance counselor or, in recent years, dean of students, or even principal. No matter the title, the purpose was to use Black staff members to address, mediate, and control problems with Black students, particularly in schools with questionable histories in fairly and equitably addressing issues of race. This often amounted to little more than window dressing as usually little was done to modify the policies and social structures that were the foundation of inequality and inequity. In my more than four decades in public school education, I know of no district that addressed, through ongoing sensitivity training, the cultural divide between White faculty and Black students.

The above scenario occurred in my first vice principalship. After one year, I moved on to a district with the internationally infamous distinction of having a swastika carved in a local cornfield. My third assignment was to a school yet in the throes of state-mandated desegregation in the year 2000. Prior to that, the schools were segregated well into the late 1990s. My fourth assignment, principal, was in the same school where I began my career in administration seven years earlier.

Tracking: Academic Segregation

One of the most widely used tools for separating students within schools is "tracking" or "ability grouping." Tracking places students in courses based on any number of criteria that purport to measure their ability to succeed given the academic rigor of the respective courses. Ironically, the common standard used for placement in tracks is standardized test scores.

Typically, New Jersey students take state-mandated assessments in the spring of each year, the scores are returned to districts in late spring, and students are scheduled into classes over the summer based on those scores. As this process plays out in districts that track, all classes end up with students who have tests scores that are within a fairly narrow range. Those with low scores may be assigned to the least rigorous classes and those with very high scores are placed in gifted and talented or advanced placement courses. Despite disclaimers of intent by boards and administration, history has it that one commonly finds a disproportionately large percentage of Black and Hispanic children in the lower level classes and disproportionately large percentages of White and Asian students in the higher level, more rigorous courses.

According to an article entitled, "Quick Takes: Tracking Decisions Change Lives, published in 2000 by the Eisenhower

Consortium for the Improvement of Mathematics and Science Teaching, opponents and proponents of tracking continue the decades old debate of the pros and cons of ability grouping. Among the criticisms are:

- Tracking disproportionately assigns students from certain ethnic and lower socio-economic groups to lower tracks.
- Tracking fosters segregation by race and class and permanently labels students.
- Politically savvy parents and those with higher incomes or more education pressure schools to put their children in high-ability tracks [often without regard to test scores].
- Parents who do not participate in the informal power relations of the school [often minority parents], or do not have the ability to take time from work to discuss scheduling with teachers, cannot advocate for their children when tracking decisions are made.
- Parents from cultures that value trusting teachers expertise might be less likely than others to push for re-assigning their children to advanced classes.
- Once assigned a track, high or low students find it nearly impossible to move either up to higher tracks or down to more appropriate levels (even if they are not doing well in higher-track classes and might do better in a less-intense class).
- A disproportionate share of resources, especially well-prepared and experienced teachers, goes to high-track classes.
- The curriculum and instruction in low-track classes are frequently dead-end and boring for both students and teachers.

The chief argument against tracking as related to the achievement gap is that it tends to deny African American students the rigorous curriculum needed to learn at the highest level and demonstrate higher achievement on standardized tests. The ironic fact that these same tests are used to justify placing Black students in lower level classes effectively locks them in a catch 22: they are placed according to test scores in classes that virtually guarantee that they will continue to score at that same level.

Cultural Compression

Within this chapter may appear what some might consider conspiracy theory. It certainly is not intended to be so. There is no clearly identifiable, grand scale, underground plan to conspire against Black children in our schools. Most American educators, I believe, are decent, compassionate, empathetic people who affirm all children's inalienable right to all that America and American schools have to offer. But among them are those who are outright advocates of insidious forms of Black-White racial separation in and out of schools, others who are architects of separation models, and yet others who are the unwitting pawns who passively make such systems work on a day-to-day basis. In doing so, they create an achievement gap where there would be none if Black and White children were on a level playing field.

Educators often recognize yet tolerate a racially biased tone that is conducive to perpetuating the gap. The longer that bias remains within the culture the more difficult it is to uproot. Every employee in every urban school had a beginning, an introduction to that culture. And no matter how gung-ho their "I'm-going-to-change-the-world" passion, the vast majority experience some level of peer pressure to adopt group values. I refer to this as "cultural compression" or the tendency to be assimilated into a culture over time by gradually abandoning personal professional values and replacing them with values of the culture. Having been desensitized, members of the culture may see problematic occurrences yet turn a blind eye to them and "don't make waves" in order to be accepted by their peers.

After retiring from public education, I occasionally served as substitute teacher in the nearby city of Trenton, New Jersey in order to keep my fingers on the pulse of public education. One of the classes that I taught was in a classroom next to that of a middle aged White male veteran teacher. One day during our common prep time, I was in my room and he in his. I overheard a conversation he was having with a colleague in which he stated with no apparent emotion that he was going to fail the whole class. I found the incident interesting and disturbing at the same time. It apparently never occurred to him (or his colleague) that if the whole class failed perhaps the problem was not fully on the shoulders of the students.

The Black Stereotype

Misconceptions embedded in the Black stereotype provide America's psychological foundation for failure to adequately and aggressively address the plight of Black children in our schools. Americans from the time of Jefferson and Monroe for a plethora of capricious reasons have held onto a demeaning caricature of peoples whose ancestors came from Africa. From the most influential of White Americans to the most simple, a significant segment of our society has always existed that believes the collective character of Black people to be unmotivated, prone to violence, and intellectually limited. This by no means is to say that the majority of Americans subscribe to this myth nor can one ascribe it to a particular segment or class of the population. But there is far too much lasting evidence, born and reborn over time, to ignore the ubiquitous belief in the black stereotype.

There is much lore that accounts for the origin of portrayals of the Black man as unintelligent, shiftless, and physically threatening. That image was advanced in American history at least as early as the excerpt from the 1781 Thomas Jefferson quote cited in Chapter 2 in his famous Notes on the State of Virginia 1782. On black intelligence, our third president wrote:

> "...Advance it therefore as a suspicion only, that the blacks, whether originally a distinct race, or made distinct by time and circumstances, are inferior to the whites in the endowments of body and mind..."

In that same timeless quote, warns Jefferson of Whites' need for wariness of the likelihood of violence by freed slaves upon them:

> "...It will probably be asked, why not retain and incorporate the blacks into the state, and thus save the expense of supplying, by importation of white settlers, the vacancies they will leave? Deep rooted prejudices entertained by the whites; ten thousand recollections, by the blacks, of the injuries they have sustained; new provocations; the real distinctions which nature has made; and many other circumstances, will divide us into parties, and produce convulsions which will probably never end but in the extermination of the one or the other race."

Blackness initiates, in many Whites, what I call the mental short circuit: a state of mind and function for Whites who freeze and digress from their normal mental state when placed in the face-to-face presence of blackness. Unaccustomed to intimate or close interpersonal dealings with Black people, they can't seem to get beyond the symbolism of black skin, stumbling over patronizing statements that allude to race, like "my college roommate was Willie Jones" (easy guess that Willie is Black), or "Do you know so-and-so," clearly alluding to another Black person, as if all Blacks know each other. This lack of ease in interpersonal relations stems from the lack of familiarity facilitated by broad-scale separation (especially residential segregation) which breeds psychological segregation.

This latter point on residential segregation is an important one in that upper income residential areas throughout America are often racially homogeneous. (It's not surprising that Pheasant Hollow, the most affluent subdivision of North Dallas, did not see its first Black resident until the new millennium.) This point is especially relevant when one considers that the political movers and shakers, workplace policy makers, and people who make day-to-day decisions that direct lives of every day Americans have little interaction with and relation to African Americans.

So deeply rooted is the Black stereotype in the minds of Americans that virtually no one is immune to the power of its suggestion, including Blacks themselves, though Blacks are less inclined to paint the entire race with the same brush. In one of his contemporary standup routines, the socially astute and brilliantly incisive comedian, Chris Rock, shockingly stated "I love Black people but I hate niggas." What Rock not-so-subtlely communicated was a distinct difference between African Americans based on character, not physical appearance. Rock went on in the routine to clarify in sobering detail the difference between the two distinct types within the Black population.

Having grown up in Brooklyn's vastly Black Bedford Stuyvesant section, Chris Rock knew on one hand there were

Blacks who held mainstream American values like the nuclear family, strong work ethic, and a healthy desire for formal education. A family of such Blacks, Rock's family, is vividly depicted in his tremendously successful sitcom, "Everybody Hates Chris." On the other hand, he witnessed Blacks who scammed to receive welfare, earned a living through crime, lived violent lives, were familiar with the revolving door of prison, and held disdain for mainstream American values.

Rock's family in some regards typifies Black Americans who have lived in the aforementioned segregated communities in Dallas and Atlanta. That experience brought them in close proximity to other Black folk, affording the opportunity to assess people as individuals and to intellectualize the nuanced spectrum of individual distinctions among their race. Rock, whose high school dropout status belied his untapped cognitive and comedic genius, no doubt saw a broad array of capabilities embodied in his "Bed-Stuy" community.

That Bedford Stuyvesant community was not unlike the South Dallas community discussed in Chapter 2. A broad range of class-based values were represented within that densely populated subdivision. With their mobility constrained by the hostility of Whites in surrounding subdivisions, middle class, upwardly mobile, ethically and morally upright Blacks were forced to live in close proximity to people who lived risky life styles and invoked fear and repugnance.

Many Whites, on the other hand, have lived in segregated communities and have been brainwashed with the degrading stereotypical fables borne by the media (remember Willie Horton). Having seen countless episodes of televised crime dramas, where the criminal, drug dealer, pimp, gang banger, or prostitute are nearly always Black, Whites have been quietly indoctrinated into accepting a monolithic view of a whole race of

Black people. These same people are local community power brokers who set our schools in motion in a manner that mirrors the values of our greater society. And the policies they enact bifurcate the paths of Black and White through the benign racism embedded in the sorting processes of discipline codes, student scheduling, and other similar structures.

Personal Awakening

As the former principal of two middle schools in two New Jersey districts, I speak with first-hand knowledge and substantial anecdotal evidence of many stakeholders' unwillingness to embrace full racial integration inside school walls. All of the students arrive together at school at the same time each day. But once inside the school walls, the sorting by race begins in ways that are entirely lacking in subtlety.

In the year 2000, I fulfilled an aspiration that was 24 years in the making when I accepted the position of principal at a Monmouth County, New Jersey school that I will call FMS. At the time, the school was 40% African American, 48% White, and 12% Hispanic. Having previously taught in the nearly all-Black urban district of Newark, New Jersey and the equally Black middle class district of Willingboro, New Jersey, and having witnessed rampant substandard achievement among those students, I had long developed a passion for working with adolescents to elevate achievement. FMS, with its small, diverse, 400-student population presented the ideal laboratory for such work. However, cursory investigation of the district indicated that the position would not be without its challenges.

FMS combined in contiguous buildings with an elementary school to constitute a complex. The two schools shared some facilities like the cafeteria and gymnasium. With the elementary school housing pre-K to grade 5 and FMS housing grades 6 through 8, the physical layout and overlapping schedules made it easy for me to interact with all students of both schools. It was also easy because I have a natural affection for the little ones and occasionally visited and interacted with them at their lunch times. Not infrequently in these excursions would a strange kindergarten child tug on my pants leg and hand me a carton of milk or ketchup packet to open, no words spoken. They inducted me into their family despite the fact that I was not officially part of their school administration. It was a great human experience.

At the same time, it pained me to know that some of the elementary teachers did not have the same God-granted affection and caring for these children, especially those of color. I too often witnessed burned-out elementary teachers shouting at their charges for miniscule offenses. Reports to my counterpart of such teacher behaviors fell on deaf ears ostensibly because she too ruled with an iron hand and did so with the blessings of our equally fire-tongued female superintendent. It was no wonder that some children who entered kindergarten wide-eyed and eager came to my grade 6 less than enthusiastic about school and fully aware of the disadvantages of blackness in public school.

On one occasion early on when I visited an elementary lunch, a cute little African American girl motioned for me to come to her and to bend down so she could whisper. She said, "I'm so glad you're Black." It was poignant experiences like these that compelled me to devote due diligence to leveling the playing field for all children, regardless of color, wherever my profession took me. It also presented living evidence of the research that says race-consciousness begins around age 4. It becomes increasingly more acute at each succeeding grade level, with elements in the child's environment contributing to his or her self-image.

At FMS, I was very pleased to inherit a fairly young, mostly tenured faculty of 37 teachers with 8 support staff. I soon found them to be a close-knit group of dedicated professionals who were supportive of each other and of me as their new principal. I had heard many stories from a variety of sources about my predecessor, whose demeanor was frequently described as dictatorial, repressive, verbally abusive, and even publicly apoplectic with teachers. In contrast, my management style can be characterized as humanistic, collaborative, and promotive of professional and personal growth of those under me. In my first year, I was able to set a tone that transitioned the culture toward what I felt would be a healthier place.

My leadership philosophy requires leaders newly introduced into an existing school culture to demonstrate respect for that culture. They are outsiders until they earn entre to that social order. This ethos demands moving slowly but deliberately in rebuilding those structures or other aspects of the culture that require reworking. Principals and superintendents who come in like gang busters creating change for the sake of change may intend to promote themselves but they do little to effect lasting positive change.

I believe good leaders first study the internal and external social environments, beliefs, values, and support structures of a school culture and dismantle early on only that which is obviously detrimental to the goals of the school and the good of the students. To disregard this axiom may well hasten a new principal's demise since New Jersey affords them little protection in the first three years. This need to proceed with caution was especially applicable to FMS, which at the time of my arrival had never had an African American principal and which, in the year 2000, had not yet been released from state-mandated desegregation.

Following my own advice, I moved slowly and by the end of my first year had laid the psychological foundation among stakeholders for raising the Grade Eight Proficiency Assessment (GEPA) scores (at the time, GEPA was the only New Jersey state test in middle school). I did this by advancing an accountability-for-all mindset. I believe my teachers embraced the concept because I held myself accountable as well as them. We were in this together. I was responsible for establishing a safe school and facilitating and supporting an excellent instructional program. Their part of the contract was to provide excellent instruction and to cultivate student learning. We shared responsibility for developing a cutting edge curriculum.

Our work was indeed cut out for us as in 2000 only 14.6% of FMS's African American students had passed the previous GEPA math test while 76% of their European American counterparts passed. Upon discovering these statistics, I felt it phenomenal that I appeared to be the only one bowled over by these woefully pathetic numbers. It seemed as if other stakeholders found the huge Black-White test score gap to be normal, intractable, and untreatable.

My family's humble beginnings in the projects of New Brunswick, New Jersey, and my own success in academic settings underpinned a solid belief in the immense yet untapped, often squandered abilities of children of color. I was troubled that these children had obviously not had the kinds of opportunities and guidance that would lead to academic success. I also felt strongly that many of their teachers previously expected them to fail and approached their lessons with effort commensurate with low expectations.

The first two years at FMS greatly informed my foundation of why, in a global sense, the achievement gap exists at all as well as why it narrows then stalls. I postulated that a culture of low expectations and other deleterious factors (like student absences and long term or frequent substitute teachers) conspired to produce a substandard student knowledge base in reading and mathematics. Conversely, I assumed that Black students were capable of higher performance on tests if afforded opportunities to review skill sets missed in earlier grades.

To attack low math scores, I revised the building schedule and implemented a strategy wherein all students, grades 6 to 8, received two periods of math each day. The first class was remedial and the second kept pace with the student's grade level. The remedial class was based on the assumption that the students had simply missed skill sets somewhere along the line. The other class kept them on pace with the grade level curriculum. In the final analysis this strategy worked amazingly well. At the end of year three, that 14.6% passing for Black students became 40% passing.

Lack of Academic Rigor in Black Student' Schedules

At FMS and other New Jersey schools, there seemed to be a ceiling to Black students' improvement as none of them scored in the advanced proficient range (highest of the three test score ranges) on the state test. Given that the GEPA assesses knowledge, I hypothesized that those students of color who potentially could have scored in the advanced proficient range failed to do so due to lack of exposure to an appropriately rigorous, advanced curriculum. I also knew that historically no African American students were scheduled into gifted and talented classes. It turned out that getting them there really was a catch 22 situation in that by policy, test scores were the main factor that placed students into the Gifted & Talented (G&T) program; or so I thought.

One day a somewhat distraught Hispanic mother came to visit me. She was at wits end over her sixth grade daughter, Julia's (not her real name), plummeting grades. I pulled Julia's file and found that she had never gotten a grade below B throughout elementary school and her standardized test scores (Terra Nova) were above the 93rd percentile. But she was in all regular classes. Concerned that this bright child was falling through the cracks, I pulled the files of all students in the gifted & talent program. I was shocked to discover that two G&T children of politically empowered district-elite parents had scores in the 50th-60th percentile range while Julia was excluded though her test scores were stellar.

Further research determined that Julia was not alone as many other children of color would no doubt have been successful in the G & T program if given the opportunity. It was when I attempted to right this wrong that "all hell broke loose," to use the colloquial phrase.

My experience at FMS and like experiences as principal of the suburban Trenton school demonstrated unequivocally that there are those who would deny Black children entre to gifted & talented and advanced placement programs and the gap-narrowing rigorous instruction that they provide simply because they are the wrong color or perhaps the wrong class. Equally sad are the dynamics of this problem.

Having digested the career-threatening dangers of integrating all-white G&T classes in FMS, I cautiously took a different but equally persistent tack to integrating G&T in suburban Trenton. Some readers might ask why tread at all on this ground given the potentially high personal cost. To that I posit that "to whom much is given, much is required." All morally upright people must weigh success against greatness. The price of the former is to make no waves and endorse the status

100

quo with a promise of personal, career, and pecuniary gain. But the price of greatness is sacrifice. For educators, it requires courageous, selfless service to our students. When we consider that the life chances of children have been entrusted to us, there should be no vacillation when choosing greatness.

G & T Exclusivity as a Cultural Value

I accepted appointment to the suburban Trenton principalship on the heels of successes at producing statistically significant narrowing of the Black/White achievement gap in math and reading in my previous district. I envisioned that my school's racial test score gap and near 50-50 Black/White student population presented an exciting opportunity, laboratory if you will, to replicate earlier successes. My strategy was research-based and really quite simple: to offer the academic rigor of the G&T program to a broad racial cross section of students whose test scores were slightly below the required range for admission to the program (97th to 99th percentile) but who demonstrated a strong work ethic and desire to achieve scholastically. These students are easily identified vis a vis their regular attendance and excellent homework completion history.

When I created opportunities for qualified African American students to be admitted to G&T classes in the suburban Trenton school, several of the white students, who had been together in advanced classes since elementary school and formed a loose academic cohort, immediately took notice and apparent umbrage. Subsequently, these students went home and discussed the "intruders" with their parents who then, after meeting and sharing notes, stormed the superintendent's office (who was also African American) and pounced full force upon him about the issue.

Given the confidentiality of student records, the group of white parents had no knowledge of the Black children's qualifications, only that they clearly thought the G&T classes were their private domain. The assumption was that the African American students did not belong. The G&T policy (previously written by the Black superintendent) gave grading and test score guidelines for admission but did not mandate strict adherence to criteria. Moreover, no student was excluded who "belonged" there but others were added that I, as principal, felt to be capable of success in the program and who earned the right to try.

But the greatest justification for infusing so-called "unqualified" Black children into the highest level classes was the fact that their less-than-perfect test scores were not of their own making. These children had been summarily placed in curricula that lacked the rigorous subject matter necessary to achieve at the highest level *yet they nearly got there anyway*. This constituted an injustice long overdue for correction. We righted this wrong and the results were nothing short of amazing.

Results of a Great Experiment

The African American children ultimately proved themselves worthy of entre into the G&T program. A statistical T test using first marking period data from newly-added Black children and old White students identified the Black children as a separate group from the Whites. However, I was delighted to find that the second marking period T test results indicated that all of the children, Black and White, were from a single population. The children, as a subgroup, were elated at being named to G&T and had risen to the occasion. I hypothesized that their lower first marking period grades were due to less rigorous prior year curricula of the subgroups. Essentially, it took only one marking period for them to catch up. Thereafter, they pulled their own weight and kept a learning pace with their White counterparts.

The greater significance of this simple experiment should not be lost on the reader as we reflect on Dr. Claude Steele's theory of stereotype threat and its possible link to poor test performance (Steele, 1999). My informal experimental subgroups in the suburban Trenton G&T classes as well as subgroups in a controlled formal study of the Jackson Homework Motivator contradict Steele's assertion and show the limited generalizability of Steele's stereotype effect on academic performance.

As discussed in Chapter 2, Steele found that Black students, when engaged in test settings with White students, were intimidated by the lower intellectual expectations of Blacks inherent in the black stereotype in general. This situational fear essentially disabled their normal abilities and they performed relatively poorly as a result. Though my practice-based experiment could not hold up to the clinical rigor required by Steele's experiment and clinical research in general, it is undeniable that the suburban Trenton Black students were not the least bit intimidated by the challenge of being placed in a more rigorous curriculum alongside White children. They accepted the challenge and in several classes actually attained a reverse achievement gap wherein Black students outperformed Whites.

The results of the aforementioned informal controlled experiment were even more successful than I envisioned at its inception. Using powerful comparative statistics, I demonstrated after only one semester that the Black students had risen to the level of or surpassed their White counterparts despite having "not qualified" for the G&T program (their prior test scores were in the 88th to 92nd percentiles). Unfortunately, the political backlash was tremendous from White parents accustomed to a virtually all white G&T program. On the heels of political pressure from those parents, the superintendent felt compelled to return to strict adherence to policy and required that only students who scored in the 97th to 99th percentiles be admitted into G&T.

A Brief Testing History

The stringent, restrictive policy guidelines for admission into the above gifted and talented program are replicated in thousands of suburban districts throughout the United States. In fact, socially-conservative American leaders have long recognized the utility of standardized test scores as an ostensibly objective means of segregating the highest level curricula in favor of White students. The rationale is simple: AP and G&T courses advance the rigorous, challenging content that best prepares students for high stakes tests and ultimately the finest colleges and universities. The traditionally poor schooling afforded the masses of Black students virtually assured that they would be ill prepared for achieving high test scores and competing for university seats.

As early as the late 1940s, influential conservative Whites like South Carolina's David W. Robinson foresaw a shift in America's social landscape. With World War II having drawn to an end, Black soldiers, having fought valiantly in segregated armed forces, refused to return home to the second class citizenship that America's segregated society promised. A movement was afoot within the Black population that demanded access to the American dream, including opportunities in higher education found primarily in historically white universities.

Due to the South's court-endorsed, separate-but-equal doctrine, southern Blacks had long been educated in public schools grossly lacking in the attributes required for preparation for higher education when compared to white public schools. Armed with the common knowledge of the inferiority of Black schools, Robinson, an attorney by profession, proposed subjecting Black and White students to rigorous content-based entrance exams. The outcome was predictable as Blacks were legally excluded from South Carolina's white universities based on test scores.

The above is a sad commentary on America's lack of willingness to depart from racist cultural values and beliefs that perpetuate the achievement gap. There is no credible research that proves Black students are any less intellectually capable than any other racial group. In New Jersey and nationally, they are underrepresented in gifted & talented and AP classes, overrepresented in special education and basic skills classes, and disproportionately appear on discipline rolls. Sadly, this pattern has become symbolic and accepted. All children need a forum in which their God-given talents can be exercised and embraced. Since the public schools are where good Americans are made, schools should provide just such a forum.

<u>White Privilege and the Schools</u>

Reflecting back on Chapter 2, a vivid image was portrayed of Alabama Governor George Wallace taking on the United States Attorney General Nicholas Katzenbach in a pitched battle of the Southern tradition of segregation in public schools versus the Supreme Court-ordained right of Black children to attend those same previously all-White schools. The issue was more than Black kids sitting next to Whites in classrooms. It was about equity and quality of schools. It was about shabby, under-equipped, poorly staffed black schools and resultant substandard education versus well-equipped white schools with highly credentialed teachers who produced promising life chances for White children.

The above was by no means confined to Alabama, Mississippi, and the other states below the Mason-Dixon Line. It was played out, albeit with less rancor and greater stealth, throughout the United States in areas without codified traditions of outright separation of the races. While there certainly were pockets of equity and opportunity to be found in many schools in American communities, more than 100 years after the Emancipation Proclamation, Black children were continually placed in a social holding pattern derived from substandard schooling.

All this begs the question of how such a pervasive injustice could prevail over such an extended period of time despite the gradual removal of legal and social policy structures that facilitated segregation. What unseen forces remained in place although tangible structures supporting inequity disappeared? The answer lies partly in the social advantage and psychology of White Privilege.

Education and Social Mobility

In a now-famous speech made in the fall of 1883, Frederick Douglas spoke on the plight of the freed Black man in America as he shed the shackles of slavery only to increasingly encounter a new set of constraints that were economic and social in nature. Douglas said:

> "Though the colored man is no longer subject to barter and sale, he is surrounded by an adverse settlement which fetters all his movements. In his downward course he meets with no resistance, but his course upward is resented and resisted at every step of his progress."

Though Douglas was addressing a social context that existed more than 100 years ago, his words sadly ring true at the turn of the second millennium as Black Americans continued to be met by glass ceilings in many avenues of life including employment and public education.

The historic failure of African Americans to join the melting pot is deeply rooted in the worldwide belief that American Blacks are permanently relegated to the lowest of social positions, American pariahs, if you will. Indeed, even as new Europeans, Asians, and Hispanics migrate to America, each population is able to achieve economic growth, and thus improved social status, at a rate greater than the masses of Black Americans. An excellent example is found in the case of Mexican Americans. The 1990 U.S. census totaled their numbers at 13.5 million, a 54% increase since the 1980 census. In 1990, the African American population was at 30 million, an increase of 12% since 1980 (www.census.gov). Yet despite their relative newcomer status to our country, Mexican Americans' household income stood at $34,000 in 2004 as compared to $30,000 for African Americans (US Census Bureau, 2005).

These data suggest better progress for the children of non-black minorities and raise questions about the plight of Black children, who are well aware of their position as social bottom-dwellers. A reflection of this can be seen in the trends in academic achievement of both groups as measured by standardized test scores of the past three decades (see Tables 1 and 2, page 11). The phenomenon wherein children of new "voluntary" American immigrants of color outstrip those of "non-voluntary" Americans of color in terms of academic success and subsequent social mobility has been the subject of some study (Suarez-Orozco & Suarez Orozco, 2001; Fordham & Ogbu, 1986).

One common denominator of both groups is their participation in the public school experience, where each is thoroughly inculcated with Eurocentric American cultural values and beliefs. However, whereas voluntary immigrants most often embrace traditional American values and have them reinforced in the home, many African American children tend to repel the same (Fordham & Ogbu, 1986) and experience teaching within the home and their communities that encourages wariness of White people and things symbolic of whiteness.

The time-honored relegation of Blacks as socioeconomic bottom-dwellers has strengthened over time in large part because it is not a priority of American policymakers to remove old economic and social fetters borne by African Americans. Quite the contrary, as old shackles appear to be removed they are frequently replaced by new, shinier, more insidious, often more substantial ones that in due time are revealed as ineffective pacifiers in which intended purpose and results are diametrically opposed. Such is often the case with public education. Presented as a vehicle in which all children can be educated and as the foundation upon which the American dream is constructed, public schools have become a primary tool through which Eurocentric social values have imparted a sense of racial strata into the psyches of children – and thus adults.

Compelling proof of the adverse effects of segregation in America public schools on Black children was advanced by Black psychologists Kenneth and Mamie Clark in the 1930s and 1940s. The Clarks conducted scientific studies on young children's self-perception by using Black and White dolls to gain insights into Black girls' racial beliefs. The subjects were given dolls that were identical in every way except for skin and hair color. One doll was white with blond hair as the other was brown with black hair. When asked to identify the "bad" or "good" doll and the "pretty" or "ugly" doll, a statistically significant sample chose the White doll as good and pretty and the brown doll as bad and ugly. The Clarks' experiment was replicated in cinema by Kiri Davis in 2005 with similar results: Black children demonstrated an unhealthy sense of self-worth when compared to White children. (abagond.wordpress.com/2009/05/29/the-clark-doll-experiment/).

The same societal elements that impact Black children's self-image in a negative way may well do the reverse for White children given the pervasive existence of white privilege in America. Television and cinema, for example, are two American institutions that commonly portray Whites in a positive light and Blacks in a negative one. Thus, a simple experiment like the above Doll Test demonstrates that as early as age 4, children develop a sense of race and racial preference. By grade 4, many White students in segregated G&T classes may develop a sense of privilege and racist attitudes about Black children's intellect and worthiness to be in advanced classes.

My experience has been that suburban school boards, administrators, and scheduling personnel, usually guidance counselors or administrators, often accommodate racist attitudes and yield to white parents' desires for G&T exclusivity out of fear of white flight and its resultant shift in demographics, i.e. proportionally larger black student populations, and all it symbolizes.

I found it phenomenal that in 2004 in my suburban Trenton district, formal and informal strategies were undertaken by the board and central administration to stem white flight and retain White children at the middle school level. I challenge the reader to identify a single suburban district anywhere in New Jersey (indeed the Nation) that has attempted to stem "Black flight" through strategies of appeasement to Black parents and students.

In order to escape the perceived problems of illegal enrollment of large numbers of Black students from neighboring cities, suburban districts extend themselves to extraordinary lengths to identify and screen out those who encroach in order to seek a better quality education. An extreme example of said encroachment and the fervor it generated lies in the 2012 case of Ms. Kelly Williams-Bolar, a Black single Ohio parent who was jailed and fined for enrolling her two children in a high-performing district where her father, not she, resided (huffingtonpost.com/2011/01/27/).

Throughout New Jersey and America, there are countless school districts where policymakers, boards of education, empowered elite, administrators, teachers, parents and students have perpetuated a culture of white privilege and black suppression where students of color are negatively stereotyped, pilloried, and marginalized, resulting in relative failure on standardized tests. Due to racially bifurcated systems of education, the same African American students are then stigmatized by test scores.

Abundant research and copious literature demonstrate that the Black-White achievement gap need not exist. The findings of that research present compelling arguments that Black children are no less intellectually capable than other ethnic groups; that given the opportunity they perform at least as well as other children in academic endeavors; that well-trained, dedicated, empathetic teachers can engage even the most recalcitrant students; and that energetic, committed administrators and school boards can refashion district and school cultures that foster success for all children regardless of race, family income, or community demographics.

CHAPTER FIVE:

RECONFIGURING AMERICAN SCHOOLS FOR EQUITY AND EQUALITY

> "I have never encountered any children in any group who are not geniuses. There is no mystery on how to teach them. The first thing you do is treat them like human beings and the second thing you do is love them." Dr. Asa Hilliard (www.quotesdaddy.com)

Reduced to its simplest terms, the Black-White achievement gap can be presented in terms of mathematics and statistics. Federal and state standardized test results may be divided into three levels: students who fail, those who pass, and those who pass with honors. More specifically, New Jersey's test results historically have been categorized as partially proficient (a euphemism for failure), proficient (met standard range), and highly proficient (student passed with honors). The numbers of Black and White students whose results fall into each category are then compared statistically as percentages.

We now know that Blacks' test scores on average long have fallen below those of their White counterparts. In attacking the gap, the task before us is to think outside the box in terms of powerful strategies that effectively bump Black underperforming students up into the next higher level in such a way as to make the average racial differences statistically non-significant. Such strategies do exist but they are merely words on paper in the absence of the thorough top down introspection and commitment to action required of those charged with abolishing racial differences in learning.

Efforts to close the achievement gap must begin with renewal of the minds of those who run our schools. For there is much correlated evidence that those who have led our public schools have taken a deficit view of their Black student populations. That view derives largely from the black stereotype, which characterizes Blacks as unintelligent, academically unmotivated, and prone to violence, among other negative attributes: a guilty until proven innocent proposition. Schools thus have been structured in policy and culture to accommodate that stereotype. Attacking the gap requires turning 180 degrees away from this institutionalized racism and creating a tone that celebrates the natural talents and exuberance that God gave *all* children, regardless of skin color, ethnic background, or social class.

    Establishing broad-based equity in public schools means creating school cultures that celebrate and promote high learning and family-like social interaction for all students. The gap is glaring evidence that this has been sorely lacking wherever there has been a long-standing racial divide in academic achievement. One need only examine the overrepresentation of Blacks in special education, virtual abandonment of required homework in urban schools, spate of zero tolerance discipline policies, and underrepresentation of Black students in G&T and AP curricula in mixed-race districts to underscore the veracity of this hypothesis. Comparing efficacious wealthy, white, upper class districts to struggling Black and poor districts in the aforementioned academic and policy areas is like comparing night to day.

    One reason that I have met with great success in narrowing the achievement gap in the schools in which I have been principal lies in the fact that, unlike in schools that have failed their black student populations, I have made several _positive assumptions_ about Black students and have built those assumptions into school culture, including policy and regulations:

- Assumption #1: Black students are just as intellectually talented as any other students and are capable of performing at the highest academic levels.

- Assumption #2: When motivated, Black students' academic and social behaviors will demonstrate that they "buy into" the importance and usefulness of school as a means to productive life paths.

- Assumption #3: Black students are no more violence-prone than any other racial group.

- Assumption #4: Homework is a useful tool for developing positive attitudes about school, building work ethic, reinforcing learning, and mimicking high level career responsibilities.

All stakeholders - boards of education, students, teachers, administrators, and parents - have a role in narrowing and ultimately closing the Black-White achievement gap. But the ball most certainly is in the court of boards, administrators, and teachers. Unfortunately, this viewpoint has not been widely held by administrators and teachers, who have long blamed parents for their children's failure. To those who blame parents I pose the question, "Now what?" If, for four decades, educators have adopted the position that Black parents, as a class and for whatever reasons, do a poor job of orienting their children to school, is it not the responsibility of school personnel to mount strategies to motivate children to succeed? The answer is a resounding, "Yes! Of course it is!" It is incumbent upon educators to pick up the slack created by parental ignorance, indifference, etc. They are their students' keepers! If educators don't supplement parents' home training, our society will continue to cut off African American children's access to the American dream.

This point is made more real when we examine the circumstances of thousands of African American children who populate our cities. It is quite the norm for these children to live in a single parent home or one in which their grandparent is the parent figure. In countless cases, drug abuse, prison, and dysfunction have removed one or both parents from the home and thrust mother, grandma, or auntie into the picture as caregiver. If schools are organized, humanistic, and empathetic in their approach to these children, they can afford great stability and nurturing to urban children to supplement the training and guidance provided at home.

The Importance of Quality Control

Early in my career I had the good fortune to work for 15 years as quality control manager in the manufacturing sectors of several large corporations. I count this as a blessing in that the experience greatly impacted the generalized view I have of organizations and their products, whether they be goods or services. More specifically, all goods and services are expected to be produced to desired specifications. While the customer is the ultimate judge of quality of a product or service, prudent organizations have effective systems of quality control as a means of assuring that the product meets acceptable standards.

The role of a quality control department is to sample product, often random samples, to generate data about those products. From that sample data, inferences are made about the sum total of goods or services produced. In this regard, the field of public education differs little from the corporate community in that both have products and both collect data to make inferences about their products. The difference is that corporations use data analysis to make intelligent, informed decisions for timely corrective actions. These corrective actions take place within the production processes. Manufacturing corporations make these process corrections at strategic points in the production process *before the product is completed and released.* If they fail to do so, they waste time and money by accumulating any amount of nonconforming product. Moreover, the field may be flooded with defective product.

The above manufacturing production analogy applies very well to public education. Viewing public education through the eyes of this former quality control manager, I find that public educators are amazingly unsophisticated in terms of the amount of data that is available to them for analysis versus the amount that they actually are aware of or use. This continues to occur even as they know that their particular schools and districts have cranked out untold numbers of nonconforming product (underachieving students). America has traveled this road to the point where learning and teaching nonconformance has been the rule rather than the exception in far too many districts.

Fortunately, there is a growing cohort of American educational institutions that are especially data conscious. These educators gather information about key aspects of their academic processes, feed that information into a database, and conduct data analysis on-the-fly in order to take timely corrective actions at crucial points in the school year. That data is individualized down to the grade, classroom, teacher, and student levels in order to tailor learning programs and make timely corrective actions. Modern computer programs facilitate this process for entire student populations in such a way as to put entire classrooms, grades, and schools on the radar screen, thus preventing children from falling between the cracks regardless of parents' levels of engagement in their children's education.

Humanistic Discipline Policies

Much academic and student discipline data is available for analysis and corrective action. However, in the case of discipline, the data is too often viewed through the race-tinted lens, resulting in heavy-handed student outcomes that have proven detrimental to Black students. Excellent anecdotal evidence of this problem can be found in revisiting a glimpse at my first year as vice principal in Southern New Jersey.

Middle school vice principals are often firemen: they put out disciplinary fires all day every day. The discipline process begins with a set of rules set forth in discipline policy. Those students who commit infractions of the rules or "discipline code" are written up, usually by a faculty member, on an office referral form and that form is forwarded to the vice principal. The great opportunity presented by this scenario is that it generates a copious amount of data over time, e.g. which teachers write up which students, the nature of the infractions, information about students, information about teachers, and information about the interdisciplinary teams from which the office referrals emanate. It also generates data that can be juxtaposed to its overarching policy. Using this information, I soon discovered that while Black students comprised only 40% of my student body, 90% of the referrals involved Black students.

To contextualize this scenario for the reader, in my first year as school administrator, I was replacing a retiring African American man who held the position for many years. Neither he nor the other two administrators had ever analyzed or acted upon the rich data generated by office referrals in order to address the obvious teacher-student racial divide; a divide in the school that was made apparent by the nature of the referrals.

A classic example of data worthy of examination involves a rule found in most discipline codes relating to an offense called "defiance of authority." Strongly subjective in tone, this offense gives teachers broad latitude in interpreting Black children's countenance, body language, vocal tone, or no behavior at all (e.g., "I told him to sit down but he didn't move fast enough."). In the absence of cross-cultural understanding between teacher and student, the student is often written up and a paper-trail begins. I strongly suspect that such misunderstandings play a major role in America's egregiously high discipline rates for Black students, especially males.

The above scenario plays out countless times in countless districts and schools across the United States. We saw in previous pages that according to published data from the U.S. Department of Education for the 2004-2005 school year, Black students in schools in 21 states were suspended at rates more than double their percentages in the student populations (nces.ed.gov/pubs2005). Those data found that in Minnesota Black students were suspended 6 times as often as Whites. In Iowa, where Blacks comprised only 5% of public school populations, they accounted for 22% of suspensions. In New Jersey public schools, African-American students were almost an astounding 60 times as likely as white students to be expelled for serious disciplinary infractions (chicagotribune.com/chi-070924discipline)

Clearly, the underlying policies that supported these statistics were not working for the betterment of African American students. To the contrary, they likely promoted anger, disillusionment, and bitterness, providing fodder for the nation's atrociously high Black student high school dropout rate.

Student behavior policies (discipline codes) should be living documents in all school districts. It is imperative that administrators remain vigilant of the social indicator data generated by such policies by regularly reviewing graphic representations of data and meeting with faculty members to address negative trends. This set of actions requires courage on the part of the administrator in that, on occasion, the end result is to require a teacher to renew the tone of his or her interactions with students.

While working as vice principal in another district, I endeavored to reduce the number of office referrals and after school detentions meted out by teachers. The first step was to weekly log the referrals generated by each teacher and distribute confidential reports to respective teachers. One particular teacher commonly generated page after page of write ups that she had handed out almost exclusively to boys.

In Chapter 2, I cited part of Dr. Ronald Ferguson's three-pronged strategy for closing the achievement gap. One leg of his Tripod Project suggests that to achieve productivity in the classroom, teachers must develop relationships with their students
(cepr.harvard.edu/ncte/news/NCTE_Conference_Tripod.pdf).
As perplexing as it may sound, disengaged students who are on the brink of failure will often work only for the teacher(s) that they admire and respect. Attaining breakthrough with such students requires some level of persistent emotional investment on the part of the teacher *even when the student is standoffish.*

Clearly that type of investment was foreign to the aforementioned teacher whose primary strategy for addressing student nonconformance was coercion via detentions and office referrals. Punishment was administered as a monotonous strategy despite its proven fruitlessness.

In Loco Parentis

Each day hundreds of thousands of parents send their children to public schools trusting that the teachers and staff of said schools will exercise much of the same care and thoughtful treatment of their children that they, the parents, put forth. Past public school law endorsed this notion in the form of a doctrine know as *in loco parentis*, Latin for in place of the parent (educational-law.org/345-in-loco-parentis). While this principle has met with legal challenges in more recent years, much of the underlying concept remains intact and has importance in approaches toward equity in our schools.

Good parents act in the best interest of their children in measures of discipline. But sometimes in parent-child conflict the parent may be misguided or even dead wrong in the manner in which the child is corrected. This situation also holds true when teachers make accusations toward students or fly off at the handle when pressed to the limit amid stressful scenarios.

After letting the dust settle, parents and teachers gain miles of respect by atoning or apologizing for the wrong done to the child. In thus doing, the teacher can make inroads with the aforementioned relationship with the student by taking a situation that would likely have made the child angry, mistrustful, withdrawn, or resentful and turning it into one in which the teacher is humanized and the child is empowered.

In contrast with the above, I implore educators to not be permissive by too often pardoning students who break rules. Organization and order require rules and children are best socialized by impressing upon them the importance of following rules. But I believe the Biblical tenet best guides us in this regard: "The Lord disciplines those he loves, as a father the son he delights in." (Proverbs 3:12). This proverb suggests that discipline should be administered with love and caring. When it is so done, children are more likely to accept it and learn from it.

Equal Opportunity to Learn: G&T and AP

Boards of education that preside over academically challenged districts, those with statistically significant racial achievement gaps, would do well to encourage lead administrators to form and maintain Achievement-For-All Committees. Membership on such committees might include a cross section of stakeholders who have the aptitude for mining and analyzing school or district social, extra-curricular, and academic data. One of their objectives would be to provide insights into statistics with embedded racial overtones.

One good example of a statistic that I discovered with embedded racial overtones can be found in New Jersey's reporting of standardized test scores. As stated earlier, test scores have been grouped as partially proficient, proficient, and advanced proficient. All students in a given district or school who took one of the ASK (now PARCC) tests, for example, had their scores placed in those groups. In doing a random, informal analysis of scores of racially diverse districts, I discovered that African Americans commonly were severely underrepresented in the advanced proficient category. In fact, in many districts it was not uncommon to find the per cent Black in that category to range from 0.0% to 3.0% even though African American students might comprise more than one third of the overall student body.

The general conclusion that I drew from the above information was that, for whatever reason, Black students had not been exposed to the rigorous content necessary to score highly on the respective ASK exams. More specifically, those students may not have been scheduled into gifted and talented or advanced placement classes, perhaps the teachers' pacing was poorly managed, maybe formative exam data was not properly used, or any combination of these circumstances.

Previously noted anecdotal evidence prompted me to investigate the extent to which Black students have been excluded from the advanced curricula that would lead to high test scores. That evidence arose in each of the two districts in which I was middle school principal. In those cases, it was determined that influential White parents exercised White privilege by exerting political pressure on the administration to keep G&T classes white. Their apparent feeling was that their children were entitled to a private school education in public school.

In Kevin Kruse's best-selling book on race in America, White Flight: Atlanta and the Making of Modern Conservatism, the author outlined the conservative movement as it aligned with segregationist politics. Kruse addressed a phenomenal sentiment within the neo-conservative movement in which Whites assert a sense of entitlement, a right, to determine the ethnic composition of their children's schools. A similar situation occurred in the Charlotte-Mecklenburg school district in the 1990s. Accordingly, boards and administrations readily and surreptitiously accommodated elitist parents by manipulating formal and informal policy such that the criteria for entrance into G&T and AP classes would generally exclude nearly all children of color.

It is this author's opinion that this thinking has influenced formal and informal G&T and AP policies that determine who gets into these powerful programs. Given that AP courses play a major role in calculating GPA and high GPA influences scholarship eligibility and college acceptance, equity dictates that districts should steer Black students as well as Whites in the direction of challenging curricula.

The aforementioned committees might take on this challenge. Standing school board-supported committees should uncover scheduling biases, thereby providing an invaluable resource for assuring equity in academic opportunities for all children, regardless of political influence or race.

Schooling as a Foot Race Metaphor

The disparate fortunes in academic achievement of Black and White American students from the latter half of the nineteenth century to present are analogous to a handicap foot race between two contestants. One contestant, the white one, is allowed to run free without encumbrances toward the goal line. The other contestant, the black one, is required to carry heavy and bulky weights during the contest. The outcome of the race is obvious, predictable, and predetermined.

This foot race metaphor is a very appropriate and telling one in portraying the bifurcated results of tests of academic progress administered to the two racial populations over the decades following the Brown decision. Initial National Assessment of Educational Progress (NAEP) exams administered in 1971 found a young Black middle school population that was marginally literate with nearly 80% reading no higher than a basic skills level (see Table 2, p. 11); this while more than 60% of White children of the same age had reading skills high enough to assure their academic success in secondary school and beyond.

At the time of the Brown decision, it was common knowledge that African American children had much catching up to do to repair the academic damage depicted by the aforementioned handicap race that took place during prior decades of poor schooling. The federal government began regular nationwide testing via the NAEP to assess the extent of that damage and to track the efficacy of various initiatives aimed at closing the Black-White achievement gap.

Throughout the previous chapters we've thoroughly demonstrated that America is at an impasse in closing that gap due in major part to her inability to live up to her melting pot promise of equal opportunity to achieve and succeed regardless of race. Through the courts, African American children had earned the right to attend the same public schools as their white counterparts. But clearly other forces were at work within the schoolhouse that hamstrung those opportunities and prevented the two races from learning, and thus testing, at similar levels.

The Value of Confidence in Learning

In 1952, at the age of eight, I watched the Rocky Marciano versus Jersey Joe Walcott fight on television with my father. From then to the present day, I've been a fan and student of the manly art of self-defense, "the sweet science," as it is known. As a fight fan I've studied the great heavyweight fighters of our time: Rocky and Jersey Joe, Floyd Patterson, Muhammad Ali, "Smoking" Joe Frazier, and, perhaps the most devastating puncher of the lot, George Foreman. While I greatly appreciated the ring skills of these men, I knew I was seeing something special when "Iron Mike" Tyson came along. At 5 feet 11½ inches tall, Tyson often had a shorter reach, the length of the outstretched arm, than many of his opponents. On paper, this put him at a disadvantage. In reality, it made little difference as Mike annihilated his first 19 opponents, winning all by knockout, 13 in the first round. He went on to become the youngest heavyweight champion in history.

A simple understanding of the fundamentals of athletics enables one to see why Mike Tyson was such an exciting and outstanding fighter; one that a fan sees but once in a lifetime. Physiologically, boxing and other sports are about speed, quickness, agility, strength, power, balance, and explosiveness.

Tyson embodied all of these in a combination not seen before him nor since him. But he was only able to take advantage of his rare abilities because he had a master teacher in Cus D'Amato, cutting edge training, extraordinary desire to succeed, great boxing intelligence, and supreme confidence. Tyson was himself a boxing historian and student of the great heavyweight fighters. His knowledge of anatomy, learned under D'Amato, was used in producing perhaps his most notable knockout when he defeated Trevor Berbick for the championship, knocking him down four times with a single punch.

In the 2006 World Tennis Association player rankings leading up to the Australian Open Championship, Russian born Maria Sharapova stood at number 2 in the world. Her opponent, Serena Williams, the great African American tennis player who had had her share of problems in 2006 was ranked number 95 (sports.espn.go.com/sports). Prior to the January 2007 tournament, Sharapova played as well as one would expect of number 2 in the world. Willams' play was another story, prompting sportswriter Pat Cash to write in his article entitled, *"Williams is lost cause..."*

> "If anybody is qualified to make deluded statements about tennis, it is a former world No 1 and winner of seven Grand Slam titles. But when Serena Williams arrives in Australia on her first foreign playing trip in a year and announces that it is only a matter of time before she is again dominating the sport, it's time to tell her to get real."
> www.timesonline.co.uk

At the outset of the tournament, Serena had not managed to be ranked among the 32 top seeded players. **Many fans likely fell into two camps: diehard Williams fans who expected Serena** to hang tough and battle her way through the rounds and Sharapova fans who expected Sharapova to win in a rout. In the final analysis, the match did end in a rout, but to the astonishment of the sports world, the Russian was on the losing end as Williams thoroughly overwhelmed the top-seeded Sharapova from the opening serve. So complete and unrelenting was Serena's dominance throughout the match that Sharapova could only manage to hold serve once in the first set and twice in the second. In the end, Serena had the last word over her detractors as she prevailed 6-1, 6-2.

A common factor in the performances of Mike Tyson and Serena Williams is that in the cited events, both played in what the sports world calls "the zone: a state of focused attention or energy so that one's performance is enhanced" (dictionary.reference.com). Beyond this simplistic definition, those who enter "the zone" in any performance endeavor are actually in a superlatively confident mental state. In my opinion, there is no factor more fundamental to achieving success than confidence in one's ability to succeed; to emerge victorious regardless of oppositional forces. This axiom is as applicable to academics as in any other context.

In the previous chapter, I made mention of a gifted and talented pilot study in which African American students were allowed to participate in my school's G&T program for the first time. By any standard, these children were excellent students yet they were denied affirmation of that fact by being placed in tracks that were below their ability levels. My pilot placed "pioneer" students with talented master teachers who accepted the responsibility, indeed privilege, of working with students who then-to-fore through no fault of their own had been denied the spiritual and emotional gold stars of placement in the highest academic courses. Simple placement of these children in G&T

was a primary factor that infused them with a greater sense of purpose and confidence. Success ensued.

As suggested in the previous chapter, the outcome of my G&T pilot flew in the face of Dr. Claude Steele's stereotype threat theory. For unlike students in Steele's racially mixed classes my African American children did not fold into underperformance but in some cases actually achieved a reverse achievement gap. By surpassing their white counterparts in scores on uniform formative and summative exams administered to all students, these middle school children rose to the occasion, validating the decision to place them in academically rigorous programs.

It should be noted here that the psychological ploy of one teacher, whom I'll call Mr. R, may have angered and inspired some students. He simply purposefully suggested to them at the outset of his classes that their previous placement in a lower track was due to in large part to the G&T students being smarter than them. Having done this, his ensuing behavior stated otherwise as he exercised appropriated pedagogy, maintained rigorous pacing, and introduced content that was high on Bloom's Taxonomy. Individualized homework followed problems identified on his frequent formative exams. In short, his demonstrated belief in his students' abilities belied his opening statement, shoring up their belief in themselves and igniting confidence like they had not experienced before. He facilitated placing his students in an academic zone.

Reinforcement and Acceleration

There are any number of instructional interventions that can boost learning and academic test scores but instructional reinforcement is perhaps the most effective and powerful. This point was dramatically demonstrated and underscored in Mr. R's classroom. His students had known success and likely felt confident on a lower academic track but their placement in the G&T program represented a steep step up. That is where Mr. R's skill as a master teacher enabled the spiking of his student's confidence even though the content and pace were appreciably more rigorous.

Research substantiates the high expectations placed in the above pilot. According to statistical meta-analyses performed by Dr. Herbert Walberg on effects of instructional factors on student learning, reinforcement was found to be the most powerful by far in elevating learning and thus student test scores. Acceleration was determined to be a close second behind reinforcement (Walberg, H.J., 1984). Dr. Walberg and colleagues synthesized nearly 3000 studies of the effects of instructional factors on student outcomes. The results of their work was expressed in effect size of each intervention and matching end percentile resulting from the intervention. Gall, Borg, and Gall (1996) adapted Walberg's work into a table.

The meta-analyses performed by Walberg (1984) and Wang et al (1993) highlight controlled studies in which instructional interventions were given to students who had scored in the 50th percentile on tests of learning in various content areas. Outcomes of those interventions were measured at the end of given instructional periods. According to the findings of the studies, students who had received lessons designed around a foundation of instructional reinforcement grew in achievement from the 50th percentile to the 88th percentile. Likewise, those receiving an intervention based on acceleration progressed from the 50th to the 84th percentile (Gall, M.D., Borg, W.R., Gall, J.P, 1996). It may be noted here that instructional interventions centering on graded homework enabled students to progress to the 79th percentile.

Educators intending to focus on improving achievement to a statistically significant extent are encouraged to mount strategies such as these that are carefully crafted and firmly based in the bountiful research that is at their fingertips. Packaged strategies should be carefully examined before adoption and teachers should be well trained and invested.

Accountability for All

Standardized tests –ASK, HSPA, AP, and SAT in New Jersey - are referred to as "high stakes" tests. It is a most accurate and ominous phrase, for these test scores greatly impact children's short and long term futures. On the line are which courses they'll be placed in; which academic tracks they'll be assigned to; whether or not they'll be relegated to advanced curricula or be assigned to the academic black holes of special education or basic skills; whether they graduate and which colleges will accept them; whether or not they'll be eligible for scholarship monies; and, ultimately, the quality and gainfulness of their future employment. Indeed, "high stakes" is an understatement for the masses of America's Black children as the test scores associated with each individual will follow him or her in a computer file in perpetuity as the achievement gap data strongly correlates with higher Black unemployment, lower average family income, and lower Black family wealth (cepa.stanford.edu/sites/default/files/reardon...; iasp.brandeis.edu/pdfs/Author/shapiro-thomas...).

Using students' test scores as primary indicators of school system efficacy camouflages and gives anonymity to the professionals responsible for producing the substandard product in systems where failure has been ongoing. In fact, my experience has been that most schools would be hard pressed to statistically quantify a given teacher's competence or incompetence in terms of value added to their students over time. Yet, for those teachers and administrators there are no high stakes tests. For them there are no stigma-laden, career debilitating test scores in their files. They are one half of a paradoxical system that stigmatizes the client for the incompetence, indifference, and/or negligence of the education practitioner.

It is for this reason that I advocate adoption of a value-added formula and system for measuring teacher and administrator efficacy. It's really quite simple. With the modern evolution of standardized tests, in many states each successive year's test correlates statistically with the previous year's test. New Jersey was a prime example with its ASK series (though they will be back at square one with the introduction of PARCC).

I suggest computer tracking the scores of students in each classroom from year to year. The previous year score serves as pretest and year end as posttest scores. Considering other factors like student attendance, test score growth can be used to calculate a given teacher's statistical effect size, or rating. The sum total of teacher ratings in a given school serves as the principal's rating.

To those who think this to be absolute heresy, I say that from 2001-2006 I used a rudimentary form of this system as a New Jersey principal and it worked very well. It's not a "gotcha" tool where administrators point fingers at teachers but one that fairly quantifies the teaching-learning process and includes the principal as chief academic facilitator. Low teacher effect sizes suggest the need for principal-teacher collaboration on a multi-pronged plan for instructional improvement, with the administrator serving as quality control manager. In the final analysis, students benefit from such a system in that all, not just students, are under the looking glass and stakes are equally high for all.

President Obama's Minority Male initiative

As this book was being completed, President Barack Obama elicited the commitment of 60 of the nation's largest urban school districts in improving the lot of African American and Hispanic boys. The large scale effort sought to:

- expand quality preschool access;
- track data on black and Hispanic boys so educators can intervene as soon as signs of struggle emerge;
- increase the number of boys of color who take gifted, honors or Advanced Placement courses and exams;
- work to reduce the number of minority boys who are suspended or expelled;
- increase graduation rates among African-American and Hispanic boys.

The effort is packaged in a part of the president's My Brother's Keeper program, which is aimed at encouraging grass roots support for Black boys. The program was organized on the heels of data that highlighted the urgent need for assistance to at-risk young males.

The Obama proposal affirmed the need for this book. Whereas the text of his initiative has been written in politically-correct terms, this writer has avoided such tact in large part due to widespread denial of the depth of the race issue in our country. For most white Americans, I believe lack of sensitivity to the issue is due in large part to the insulation provided by superficial interpersonal relationships with Blacks. This condition plays out especially with teachers.

Data included in Chapter 4 suggests that in the cases of urban and urban rim schools, the majority of teachers are White females who teach Black children that they see daily but know only on a superficial level. They live in different neighborhoods, belong to different social classes, and have minimal interracial interaction occurring outside of school. In fact, my experience has been that despite the great teacher-student connection value found in home visitations, White teachers avoid visiting Black neighborhoods out of sheer fear. I've even seen this practice discouraged by a local teachers union.

If the gap is to be closed, three conditions must be met. Teachers must first abolish stereotypical notions about Black students and replace them with positive assumptions that depict their charges as intellectually capable and full of potential. They must abandon the parent blame game and take their students as they come. If they lack motivation, find a pathway to inspiration. This is part of the teacher-student connection of which I wrote.

The second requirement for teachers in narrowing and closing the achievement gap is to be firmly in possession of appropriate pedagogic methods; methods that get the job done. In this case, there is no one-size-fits-all method. I've witnessed teachers who are firm, seemingly hard-nosed aficionados of old school direct instruction. But it worked and their students were successful.

The final piece to the achievement gap puzzle is content; rigorous content. Standardized tests are content-based and high success is derived from high, rich content taught in the classroom. But content does not stand by itself in this tripartite solution. Content must be married to pedagogy through proper pacing and frequent formative testing. Formative testing dictates instructional spiraling in order that critical content is retained by the student. Research has shown this to be a problem in our cities as teachers fail to pace instruction and content, thereby, allowing students to fall further behind with each successive year. This problem has been exacerbated by the insane exercise in urban schools of abandoning the standard curriculum for weeks on end in order to teach and practice the test.

In conjunction with the above tripartite strategy for closing the gap, PARCC is an important factor that will come to fruition as this book is published. Unfortunately, I believe the concept is so new and different for most teachers that several years will pass before the system becomes fully functional and effective. But it certainly is a giant step in the right direction. Schools would do well to use PARCC as it is intended to track student progress and to abandon the old practice of using formative tests in a summative manner rather than using test data to guide further instruction.

Computerized testing plans that employ uniform exams followed by test data analysis and results-based re-teaching is a practice that has been in place by forward-thinking education systems like Sabis International. The practice has been instrumental in guiding Sabis schools' amazing success by using ongoing assessment in all content areas, monitoring of test progress, and positive intervention based on test data. This system has not only prevented students from falling through the cracks, it has boasted 90%-plus graduation rates and catapulted the majority of its graduates to four-year colleges (www.sabis.net/educational-systems/educational-approach/testing-and-monitoring).

REFERENCES

Akos, Patrick & Galassi, John P. (2004). Middle and high school transitions as viewed by students, parents, and teachers. *Professional School Counseling, 7(4)*

Alderman, M.K. (2004). *Motivation for achievement*. Mahwah: Lawrence Erlbaum Associates.

Anyon, Jean (1997). *Ghetto schooling: a political economy of urban education reform.* New York: Teacher's College Press

Barber, B. (1986). Homework does not belong on the agenda for educational reform. *Educational Leadership, 43*: 55-57

Barton, Paul E. (2003). Parsing the achievement gap: baseline for tracking progress. Educational Testing Service policy information report.

Bauerlein, Mark (2001). *Negrophobia: A Race Riot in Atlanta, 1906.* San Francisco, CA; Encounter Books

Bonczar, Thomas P. (2003). Prevalence of Imprisonment in the U.S. Population, 1974-2001, Bureau of Justice Statistics, p. 8.

Bronfenbrenner, Urie. (1979). *The ecology of human development: Experiments by nature and design.* Cambridge, MA: Harvard University Press.

Brookhart, S.M. (1997). Effects of the classroom assessment environment on mathematics and science achievement. *The Journal of Educational Research, 90:* 323-330

Brophy, Jere (2004). *Motivating students to learn.* Mahwah: Lawrence Erlbaum Associates

Brown, B.B. (1990). Peer groups and per culture. In S.S. Feldman & G.R. Elliott (Eds.), At the threshold: The developing adolescent (pp. 171-196). Cambridge, MA: Harvard University Press.

Chen, C., & Stevenson, H. W. (1989). Homework: A cross-cultural examination. *Child Development, 60,* 551–561.

Comer, J., Haynes, N., Joyner, E., Ben-Avie, M. (1996). Rallying the Whole Village: the Comer Process for Reforming Education; New York, Teachers College Press

Cook, T.D. & Campbell, D.T. (1979). *Quasi-Experimentation: Design & Analysis issues for Field Settings.* Boston, MA: Houghton Mifflin Company.

Cool, V. & Kieth, T.Z. (1991). Testing a model of school learning: Direct and indirect effects on academic achievement. *Contemporary Educational Psychology, 16:* 28-44.

Cooper, H. (1989). *Homework.* White Plains, N.Y.: Longman.

Cooper, H., Lindsay, J.J., Nye, B., & Greathouse, S. (1998).

Relationships among attitudes about homework, amount of homework assigned and completed, and student achievement. *Journal of Educational Psychology, 90*: 70-83.

Crum, C.F. (2004). Using a cognitive-behavioral modification strategy to increase ontask behavior of a student with a behavior disorder. *Intervention in School and Clinic, 39(5)*: 305-309.

Danzberger, J.P., Kirst, M.W., and Usdan, M.D. (1992). Governing Public Schools: New Times, New Requirements. Washington, D.C.: Institute for Educational Leadership.

DeMartini-Scully, D., Bray, M.A., & Kehle, T.L. (2000). A packaged intervention to reduce disruptive behavior in general education students. *Psychology in Schools, 37*:149-56.

DiMaggio, P., (1982). Cultural capital and school success: the impact of status culture participation on the grades of U.S. high school students. *American Sociology Review, 47*:189-201

Duda, J.L., & Nichollis, J.G. (1992). Dimensions of achievement motivation in schoolwork and sport. *Journal of Educational Psychology, 84*: 290-299.

Easton, J.Q., Bennett, A. (1990). Achievement effects of homework in sixth-grade classrooms. Paper presented at the Annual Meeting of the American Educational

Research Association, Boston, MA. ERIC Document Reproduction Service No. ED 320675.

Farrow, S., Tymms, P., & Henderson, B. (1999). Homework and attainment in primary schools. *British Educational Research Journal, 25*: 323-341.

Fehrman, P., Keith, T.Z, Reimers, T.M., (1987). Home influence on school learning: direct and indirect effects of parental involvement on high school grades. *Journal of Educational Research, 80(6)*:330-37

Felson, R.B. & Reed, M.D. (1986). Reference groups and self appraisals of academic ability and performance. *Social Psychology Quarterly, 49:* 103-109.

Ferguson, R. F. (2002). What doesn't meet the eye: Understanding and addressing racial disparities in high-achieving suburban schools. Cambridge, MA: Harvard University, John F. Kennedy School of Government. (ED 474 390)

Ford, Donna (1996). *Reversing underachievement among gifted black students: promising practices and programs.* New York, N.Y.: Teachers College Press.

Fordham, S., & Ogbu, J. (1986). Black Students and School Success: Coping with the Burden of Acting White. *Urban Review.*, 18(3), 176-2006.

Gall, M.D, Borg, W.R., & Gall, J.P. (1996). *Educational research: an introduction.* White Plains, N.Y.: Longman Publishers.

Gliner, J.A. & Morgan, G.A, 2000. *Research methods in applied settings: an integrated approach to design and analysis.* Mahwah, N.J.: Lawrence Erlbaum Associates

Gureasko-Moore, S.P. (2004. *The effects of self-management on organizational skills of adolescents with ADHD.* Doctoral dissertation, Lehigh University.

Harpalani, V. & Gunn, R. (2003). Contributions, controversies, and criticisms: in memory of John U. Ogbu (1939-2003). Article in *Penn Perspectives of Urban Education 1, 2(2)*

Harris, V.W., & Herman, J.A. (1974). Homework assignments, consequences, and classroom performance in social studies and mathematics. *Journal of Applied Behavior Analysis, 7*:505-19.

Herrnstein, R. J. (1973). *I.Q. in the meritocracy.* Boston: Little Brown.

Hill, W. (1985). *Learning: A survey of psychological interpretations.* (4th. Ed.).

Hong, E. & Milgram, R.M. (2000). *Homework: motivation and learning preference.* Westport: Bergin & Garvey

Hess, Frederick M. (2002). *School Boards at the Dawn of the Twenty-first Century: Conditions and Challenges of Governance.* Report prepared for the National School Boards Association.

Hwang, Y.S., Echols, C., Vrongistinos, K. (2002). Multidimensional academic motivation of high achieving African American students. *College Student Journal, 36 (4)*

Hyers, Albert (2001). Predictable achievement patterns for student journals in introductory earth science course. *Journal of Geography in Higher Education. 25(1)*, 53-66

Jacobson, N.S., Follette, W.C. & Revenstorg, D. (1984). Psychotherapy outcome research: Methods for reporting variability and evaluating clinical significance;.*Behavior Therapy, 15*:336-52.

Jencks, C. (1972). *Inequality: A reassessment of the effect of family and schooling in America* . New York: Basic Books.

Jencks, C., Phillips, M. (1998). *The Black-White Test Score Gap.* New York: Brookings Institution Press Turning Points: Preparing American Youth for the 21st century report of the Task Force on Education of Youth Adolescents

Jensen, A.R. (1969). How much can we boost IQ and scholastic achievement? *Harvard Educational Review 19*: 1-123.

Jensen, W.R., Rhode, G. & Reavis, H.K. (1994). *The tough kid tool box.* Longmont, CO: Sopris West.

Johnston, Peter (1984). Prior Knowledge and Reading Comprehension Test Bias; *Reading Research Quarterly*, Vol. 19, No. 2 (Winter, 1984), pp. 219-239

Kao, Grace & Thompson, Jennifer S. (2003). Racial and ethnic stratification in educational achievement and attainment. *Annual Review of Sociology, 29*:417-42

Kao, G., (1995). Asian-Americans as model minorities? A look at their academic performance. *American Journal of Education, 103*:121-59

Kazdin, A.E. (1982). *Single-case research designs.* New York: Oxford University Press.

Keith, T.Z. (1986). Homework. West Lafayette, IN: Kappa Delta Pi.

Keith, T.Z., & Page, E B. (1985). Homework works at school: National evidence for policy changes. *School Psychology Review, 14*:351-59.

Keith, T.Z., Reimers, T.M., Fehrmann, P.G., Pottebaum, S.M., & Aubey, L.W. (1986). Parental involvement, homework, and TV time: Direct and indirect effects onhigh school achievement. *Journal of Educational Psychology, 78:* 373-380.

LaConte, R.T. (1981). *Homework as a learning experience: What research says to the teacher.* Washington, DC: National Education Association.

Leblanc, D.B. (1998). Mystery motivator versus reinforcement: An investigation of the effects of home-based reinforcement delivery systems used with home-school notes on disruptive/disengaged classroom behavior. Unpublished doctoral dissertation, University of Southern Mississippi.

LaMorte, Michael W. (2002). *School law: cases and concepts.* Allyn and Bacon: Boston

Leone, C.M. & Richards, M.H. (1989). Classwork and Homework in early adolescence: The ecology of achievement. *Journal of Youth and Adolescence, 18(6)*: 531-48.

Madaus, Melissa M.R. (2000). Effectiveness of the Mystery Motivator intervention in improving math homework completion and accuracy percentages. Doctoral dissertation, University of Connecticut.

Madaus, Kehle, Madaus, & Bray (2003) Mystery Motivator as an Intervention to Promote Homework Completion and Accuracy. *School Psychology International; 24*: 369-377.

Maslow, A. 1962. *Toward a Psychology of Being*. Princeton, N.J.: Van Nostrand.

Miller, L.S. (1995). *An American imperative: accelerating minority educational advancement*. New haven: Yale University Press.

Montagu, Ashley (ed., 1999). Race and IQ; New York : Oxford University Press.

Moore, L.A., Waguespack, A.M., Wickstrom, K.G., Witt, J.C. & Gaydos, G.R. (1994). Mystery motivator: An effective and time efficient intervention. *School Psychology Review, 23:* 106-18.

New Jersey Department of Education Website: http://www.state.nj.us/education/

Newman-Eig, L.M. (2003). The effects of varied and constant reinforcement within an interdependent group contingency system on homework completion and accuracy rates of elementary school students. Doctoral dissertation, Hofstra University.

National Commission of Excellence in Education (1983). A nation at risk: the imperative of educational reform. Washington, DC. U.S. Department of Education.

Ogbu, J. U. (1978). *Minority Education and Caste*. New York: Academic Press

Ogbu, J. U. (1981). Origins of human competence: A cultural-ecological perspective. *Child Development, 52,* 413-429.

Ogbu, J. U. (2003). *Black American students in an affluent suburb: A study of academic disengagement.* New Jersey: Lawrence Erlbaum.

Otto, H.J. (1950). *Elementary education.* Encyclopedia of Educational Research, 2nd ed. New York Free Press.

Pascal, R.A, Weinstein, T., and Walberg, H., (1984). The effects of homework: a quantitative synthesis. *Journal of Educational Research 78*:97-104

Phillips, Michael (2006). White Metropolis: Race, Ethnicity, and Religion in Dallas, 1841-2001. Austin, TX; University of Texas Press.

Rhode, G., Jensen, W.R., & Reavis, H.K. (1992). *The tough kid handbook: Practical classroom management strategies.* Longmont, CO: Sopris West.

Robinson, K.E. (1998). Using the mystery motivator to improve child bedtime compliance. Unpublished doctoral dissertation, University of Utah.

Rosenthal, R., and Jacobson, L. (1968). *Pygmalion in the classroom.* New York: Rinehart and Winston.

Schellenberg, T., Ksok, R.L. & McLaughlin, R.G. (1991). The

effects of contingent free time on homework completion in English with senior high school English students. *Child and Family Behavior therapy, 13*: 1-11.

Skiba, Russell J., Michael, R.S., Nardo, A.C (2000). "The Color of Discipline: Sources of Racial and Gender Disproportionality in School Punishment. Policy Research Report #SRS1; University of Nebraska-Lincoln

Steele, Claude (1999). Thin ice: "Stereotype threat" and black college students. *The Atlantic Monthly, 284*(2) 44-54.

Stipek, D.J. & Gralinski, J.H. (1996). Children's beliefs about intelligence and school performance. *Journal of Educational Psychology, 88:* 397-404.

Suarez-Orozco, C., & Suarez Orozco, M. (2001). *Children of Immigration*. Cambridge, MA: Harvard University Press.

Sutton, Jeffrey S. (2008). "San Antonio Independent School District v. Rodriguez and Its Aftermath". *Virginia Law Review* **94** (8): 1963–1986.

Thernstrom, A. & Thernstrom, S. (2003). *No excuses: closing the racial gap in learning.* New York: Simon and Schuster.

Tidwell, B.J. (ed., 1993). *The state of black America.* National Urban League.

Tonglet, J.P. (2001). Influences on math homework completion and achievement: Students' attitudes toward teacher-related factors, student motivational factors, and environment-related factors in fifth and eighth graders. Dissertation Abstracts International Section A: Humanities & Social Sciences, 61 (9-A):3468.

Traitwein, U., Koeller, O., Schmitz, B. & Juergen, B. (2002). Do homework assignments enhance achievement: A multilevel analysis in 7th grade mathematics? *Contemporary Educational Psychology, 27(1):* 26-50.

Tymms, P.B. & Fitz-Gibbon, C.R. (1992). The relationship of homework to A-level results. *Educational Research, 34*:3-10.

Walberg, Herbert J., 1984. Improving the Productivity of America's Schools; Educational Leadership, 41 (8), 19-27.

Walberg, H.J. (1991). Does homework help? *The School Community Journal, 1*:13-15.

Walberg, H.J., Paschal, R.A. & Weinstein, T. (1985). Homework's powerful effects on learning. *Educational Leadership, 42*:76-79.

Wang, M.C, Haetel, G.D., & Walberg, H.J. (1993). Toward a Knowledge Base for School Learning; Review of Educational Research, 63, 249-294.

Weiner, W. (1912). Home-study reform. *School Review, 20*: 526-5231

Weinert, F.E. & Helmke, A. (1995). Inter-classroom differences in instructional quality and individual differences in cognitive development. *Educational Psychologist, 30*:15-20.

Wildman, P.R. (1968). Homework pressures. *Peabody Journal of Education, 45:* 202-204.

Will, J.C. & Martens, B.K. (1983). Assessing the acceptability of behavioral interventions used in classrooms. *Psychology in the Schools, 20*: 510-17.

Wilson, William H. (1998). Hamilton Park: A Planned Black Community in Dallas. Baltimore, MD; The Johns Hopkins University Press

Wood, Chip (1997). *Yardsticks: children in the classroom ages 4-14.* Turner Fall: Northeast Foundation.

INTERNET REFERENCES

1906atlantaraceriot.org/ Retrieved February 16, 2009. February 18, 2009.

americanhistory.si.edu/Brown/history/6-legacy/deliberate speed.html

armenianeagle.com/2007/01/26/australian-open-final-maria sharapova-vs-serena-williams/ Retrieved January 6, 2009.

boxrec.com/list_bouts.php?human_id=474&cat=boxer. Retrieved January 6, 2009

bju.edu/resources/cplanting/metro/southdallastx.html Retrieved January 18, 2009

brownvboard.org/summary/ Retrieved January 8, 2009.

weblinks3.epnet.com/ - bib9up

thinkonthesethings.wordpress.com/2007/06/02/cornel-west-on-success-vs-greatness/. Retrieved 12/30/08.

cdn.americanprogress.org/wp-content/uploads/2014/05/TeacherDiversity.pdf

cepa.stanford.edu/sites/default/files/reardon%20whither%20opportunity%20-%20chapter%205.pdf

cepr.harvard.edu/ncte/news/NCTE_Conference_Tripod.pdf).

chicagotribune.com/chi-070924discipline

civilrightsproject.ucla.edu/research/deseg/Resegregation American_Schools99.pdf. Retrieved January 5, 2009.

dallashistory.org/ retrieved January 22, 2009

dictionary.reference.com/browse/in+the+zone. Retrieved January 6, 2009.

factfinder.census.gov/ Retrieved January 22, 2009

georgiaencyclopedia.org/ Retrieved February 18, 2009.

huffingtonpost.com/2009/01/06/bush-using-federal funds_n_155734.html Retrieved January 18, 2009

leagle.com/decision/19715895Cal3rd584_1546) Grady-Willis, Winston A. (2006). Challenging U.S. Apartheid, Durham: Duke University Press.

ncaaondemand.com/clips/306101432_xxx. Retrieved January 6, 2009

nces.ed.gov/pubs2011/dropout08/app_a3.asp

nytimes.com/2014/07/21/education/obamas-my-brothers keeper-education-program-expands.html?_r=0

quickfacts.census.gov/qfd/states/13/1304000.html Retrieved February 18, 2009.

sabis.net/educational-systems/educational approach/testing-and-monitoring).

sports.espn.go.com/ncb/rankings?seasonYear=2008&weekNuber=1&seasonType=3. Retrieved January 6, 2009.

sports.espn.go.com/sports/tennis/rankings?year=2007&type=2 sport=WOMRANK Retrieved January 6, 2009.

sports.espn.go.com/sports/tennis/rankings?year=2006&type=2 sport=WOMRANK Retrieved January 6, 2009.

suspire.org/wiki/index.php/Atlanta Retrieved February 19, 2009.

timesonline.co.uk/tol/sport/tennis/article1292868.ece. Cash, Pat (2007). Times on Line, "Williams is Lost Cause" Retrieved January 6, 2009.

US Census Bureau, 2005; Median household income newsbrief

www.ingramcontent.com/pod-product-compliance
Lightning Source LLC
Chambersburg PA
CBHW071119090426
42736CB00012B/1956